The Jewish Holiday Treasure Trail

Teacher's Guide

Ellen Rank

Behrman House, Inc.
www.behrmanhouse.com
www.ElijahRocks.net

Contents

Project Editor: Dena Neusner
Book Design: Terry Taylor

The publisher gratefully acknowledges the cooperation of the following sources of photographs: Creative Image Photography 25; P. Deliss/Godong/Corbis 44; Gila Gevirtz 57, 61; Richard Lobell 8, 10, 30, 35, 48; Richard T. Nowitz/Corbis 54; Naomi Patz 20; Jeremy Poisson 15; Stockxpert 39.

Springfield, New Jersey
www.behrmanhouse.com
ISBN 978-0-87441-834-7
Manufactured in the United States of America

INTRODUCTION

The Jewish Holiday Treasure Trail invites students to follow the adventures of Daniel and Rivkah as they learn about Jewish holidays—how and why we celebrate, related history and values, and essential English and Hebrew holiday vocabulary.

STRUCTURE OF THE TEXTBOOK

In *The Jewish Holiday Treasure Trail*, Daniel, an American boy, and Rivkah, Daniel's Israeli cousin, are transported through time and space to learn about the Jewish holidays from Elijah the Prophet.

The book has thirteen chapters. Chapter 1 introduces students to the characters and storyline. Chapter 1 also features the "Treasure Trail," shown on pages 10–11, which is comprised of the Hebrew months and provides a place for students to put a sticker for each holiday as they complete the related chapter. Each of the remaining chapters is devoted to a holiday: Rosh Hashanah, Yom Kippur, Sukkot, Simḥat Torah, Shabbat (including *havdalah*), Ḥanukkah, Tu BiShevat, Purim, Passover, Yom Hashoah, Yom Ha'atzma'ut, and Shavuot.

In addition to conveying the Jewish history, *mitzvot*, and values related to the holiday, every chapter:

- Opens with a calendar showing students where the holiday falls in the Jewish year.
- Includes open-ended questions that encourage students to connect Jewish values to their daily lives.
- Recounts a classical Jewish legend or biblical account related to the holiday.
- Presents a riddle based on the holiday's customs, *mitzvot*, history, or values.
- Directs students to visit www.ElijahRocks.net where they can find key vocabulary, blessings, word puzzles, and interactive computer games that reinforce holiday words and concepts.

STRUCTURE OF THE TEACHER'S GUIDE

This Teacher's Guide is designed to help you use *The Jewish Holiday Treasure Trail* easily and effectively. It includes a variety of age-appropriate activities such as drawing, tasting foods, singing, and role-playing, which address a full range of learning modalities. This guide also offers open-ended questions you can use to stimulate critical thinking and class discussion. Throughout, it includes creative activities for family participation.

Each chapter in this guide addresses a single chapter from the textbook, using the same core structure:

- Chapter Overview: a brief statement about the chapter content
- Core Concept: the main idea in the chapter
- Learning Objectives: specific learning goals for each chapter

- Getting Started: practical suggestions for introducing the chapter
- Teaching Opportunities: teaching tips, additional information, engaging hands-on activities, and comprehension, discussion, and critical thinking questions (Where appropriate, answers are given to questions that appear in the textbook.)

Within each Teaching Opportunities section, icons identify three special lesson features:

Hands On: Activities and creative techniques help students integrate the material through, for example, art, math, movement, and food.

Family Activity: Home-based activities engage the whole family and reinforce classroom learning.

ElijahRocks: The Web site www.ElijahRocks.net provides enrichment activities for home or school. It includes interactive computer games that reinforce concepts from the book, holiday blessings, dictionaries of key holiday words, and word puzzles based on holiday vocabulary. This Teacher's Guide includes suggestions for teachers, families, and students to use the games and PDF pages found at www.ElijahRocks.net.

This Teacher's Guide provides a wide variety of activities and discussion topics. Choose the ones that best suit your classroom based on time constraints, your teaching style, and students' needs and interests.

Wishing you a year filled with wonderful holidays!

INTRODUCING YOUR STUDENTS TO THE TEXTBOOK

Introducing the Jewish Calendar: Before distributing *The Jewish Holiday Treasure Trail*, introduce your students to the Jewish calendar. Ask them to name the months of the year. *(January, February, etc.)* Explain that the months of the Jewish calendar are different. Ask your education director for a Jewish/Gregorian calendar that includes both the Hebrew and the secular month names, or print one from the Internet. Make copies of the pages for September and October and give them to your students. Have students underline *Elul* and circle *Tishre* each time these words appear on the calendar. Inform students that these are names of months in the Jewish calendar. Ask students to identify the date in Tishre when we celebrate Rosh Hashanah *(Tishre 1)* and the date in September or October this year when we celebrate Rosh Hashanah. If possible, show students a calendar from last year, and have them find the dates of the holiday for that year, too. Explain that while Rosh Hashanah may fall on September 19 one year and September 30 in another year, it always falls on Tishre 1 in the Jewish calendar. Reassure students that while this may be a bit confusing now, they will be experts in the Jewish calendar by the end of this year.

Write the following on the board: Yom Kippur; the first day of Sukkot; Simḥat Torah. Invite students to work with a partner. Ask them to refer to their calendars for this year to determine the Hebrew and Gregorian dates for each of the holidays listed on the board. *(Tishre 10; Tishre 15; Tishre 22/23)* Call on volunteers to share their findings.

Browsing Through the Book: Distribute *The Jewish Holiday Treasure Trail* to your students. Have the class read the title aloud with you. Call on volunteers to describe and identify the pictures on the cover. *(a girl holding a round ḥallah; three children looking at a havdalah candle; a dreidel; a costumed child eating hamantashen; a seder plate; a man and boy writing in a Torah scroll)* You may wish to explain that the Hebrew words and letters on the cover have the following meanings: The large letters on the seder plate spell *Pesaḥ*, which means Passover; the small letters on the seder plate spell *beitzah*, which means egg; the letters on the dreidel are *gimel* and *hay—gimel* stands for *gadol*, which means big, and *hay* stands for *hayah*, which means was or happened; the words on the wine cup are *borei p'ri hagafen*, the last three words of the blessing over wine, which mean "Creator of the fruit of the vine."

Allow a few minutes for children to leaf through the book and look at the pictures. Ask: What do you think the book is about? What are some things we might learn about? *(holidays; traditions)* Read the table of contents and have students echo the names of the holidays. Ask: Which holidays do you recognize? Which holidays are not familiar to you? *(Answers will vary.)* Show students the Treasure Trail on pages 10–11 and the stickers at the end of the book. Tell students that they will encounter riddles at the ends of chapters 2–13. Explain that each time they solve a riddle they will place the corresponding holiday sticker in its correct spot on the Treasure Trail.

TEACHING TIPS

K-W-L Chart: You may wish to create a K-W-L (**K**now-**W**ant to Know-**L**earned) chart about the holidays with your students. You can use a large sheet of chart paper or poster board for this chart. The K-W-L chart has three columns and can be used for almost any unit of study. Label the column on the left "What I Know," the middle column "What I Want to Know," and the right-hand column "What I Learned." As you study each holiday, begin by asking students what they know about the holiday and recording their responses in the "What I Know" column. Next, ask students what they would like to know about the holiday, and record their suggestions in the middle column. At the end of class, prompt students to share what they learned, and write their responses in the "What I Learned" column. You can keep this chart posted throughout the year or bring it with you and put it on the wall for each class.

Group Work: As you study the holidays, you will sometimes find it helpful to have students work together in groups. Consider creating index cards that describe the jobs of group members. Jobs will vary depending on the type of group work. Some possible jobs include the following:

- Recorder—records the group's suggestions or findings that will be reported to the class
- Reporter—reports the group's work to the class
- Illustrator—draws the group's ideas to be presented to the class
- Investigator—researches to discover information
- Encourager—encourages group members to stay on task
- Reader—reads aloud information to the group

Consider laminating the job description index cards and distributing them each time you do group work.

Hebrew Birthdays: A fun way to make the Hebrew calendar come alive for students is to celebrate the students' Hebrew birthdays throughout the year. Ask students to bring in the following information: the month, date, year, and, if possible, the time of day they were born. It's best if they can tell you the exact time because, just as Shabbat begins at sunset, the Hebrew date changes at sunset. There are a variety of tools your rabbi or synagogue should have available, such as "hundred year calendars," to calculate Hebrew birthdays. The Internet also has sites where you simply type in the English date, month, year, and time, and the English date is converted into the Hebrew date.

After determining the students' Hebrew birthdays, give each student a sticky note with the date written on it. Distribute index cards and have each student decorate a card and write his or her name and Hebrew birthday. Display all the Hebrew birthday cards on the bulletin board. Using a Jewish/Gregorian calendar, help students locate the date their Hebrew birthday falls on this year, according to the Gregorian calendar. Celebrate each student's Hebrew birthday by singing *"Yom Huledet Sameaḥ"* (Hebrew for "Happy Birthday") to the tune of "Happy Birthday to You."

Jewish Holiday Journal: Consider having each student keep a journal about the Jewish holidays. Give each student a spiral bound notebook, or help them make their own notebooks by stapling several blank sheets of paper together. Have students label the book "My Holiday Journal" and decorate the cover with illustrations of objects we use on Shabbat and other Jewish holidays. Explain that as they read *The Jewish Holiday Treasure Trail*, the students will record their thoughts and feelings about what they have learned about Jewish holidays.

For their first journal entry, ask students to record the date of their Hebrew birthday and to write or illustrate how they would like to celebrate this special day.

Teaching Students with Special Needs

Children vary in their learning styles. Some students learn best with a hands-on approach, while others do best with a visual or an auditory approach. In general, teachers who present material in many different ways will be able to reach most students.

Students with special needs, however, can have a broad range of challenges. These include cognitive, physical, and behavioral challenges that can have an impact on learning. It is always helpful to find out from families what, if any, accommodations are made for their children in secular school. The suggestions included below are primarily for those students with learning, perceptual, or attention problems.

- For students with attention and auditory processing problems, teach in small increments and present one direction at a time. Ask students to repeat the direction or explain it in their own words to be sure they have processed it.

- For students with attention problems, limit teaching segments to 10–15 minutes, and allow for movement between activities.

- For students with decoding problems, make flashcards for a few key words. Students can take the cards home for additional practice and reinforcement. Keep a shoebox of flashcards for students who need them.

- Provide opportunities for choral reading rather than asking students to read aloud individually.

- For students with attention and visual figure-ground problems, mask parts of the page so they can see only the section that is being worked on.

- For students with fine motor and handwriting problems, limit the amount of writing, drawing, and cutting that is required. Prepare these difficult parts of a project in advance of the class and have students finish the task. Allow students to use a computer when completing assignments that are typically handwritten.

- Use concrete objects whenever possible to reinforce student learning through the senses. For example, when teaching *havdalah*, bring a havdalah candle to class and have your students make spice boxes to use weekly as they recite havdalah.

You may want to make frequent use of Hebrew and English songs to teach about the holidays. (Your cantor or music specialist may be able to help you find recordings that are helpful.) Learning new songs does not incorporate writing, reading, or motor skills, and it keeps most children focused. Consider making recordings so students can hear and practice the songs at home with their families.

CHAPTER 1

Welcome to the Treasure Trail

Textbook pages 4–11

Core Concept

The Torah tells us about Elijah and the other prophets, who taught us about the Jewish holidays and the Jewish values of being kind and seeking peace.

Learning Objectives

Students will be able to:

- Identify Elijah as a prophet and name a custom associated with him.
- Recognize that the Torah teaches about holidays and Jewish values.
- List some of the holidays they will learn about during the year.
- Explain that Jewish holidays have a fixed date on the Jewish calendar.

Chapter Overview

Daniel and his Israeli cousin Rivkah travel through time and space to a virtual world called ElijahRocks, where they meet none other than Elijah the Prophet. Elijah invites them to visit the Treasure Trail, where they will learn about Jewish holidays.

Getting Started

Invite students to tell about a time when they wanted to learn more about something or how to do something new. Ask: Who did you go to for help? *(Answers may include: a dance teacher; a hockey coach; a friend who is expert at video games.)* Explain that in our book, two cousins, Daniel and Rivkah, travel back in time to meet with an expert on Jewish holidays and values, Elijah the Prophet.

Teaching Opportunities

Page 4 **Elijah:** Ask: What seder custom that includes Elijah does Daniel mention? *(We set out a cup of wine for Elijah the prophet.)* What other seder custom do you know about that involves Elijah? *(We open the door for Elijah.)* Inform students that this year we are inviting Elijah into our classroom to help us learn about the holidays and *mitzvot*.

Page 5 **ElijahRocks:** If a computer is available in your school, demonstrate for students how to go to www.ElijahRocks.net. If there is more than one computer, have students take turns going to the Web site themselves. Begin by typing www.ElijahRocks.net into your web browser. After the Web site opens, select a holiday and show students that there are blessings, vocabulary words, a word puzzle, and a computer game for almost every chapter. Tell students that they will be going to www.ElijahRocks.net throughout the year. Alternatively, write down the full web address for students to take home, and encourage them to visit the Web site at home.

Photo Op: Ask students to describe what they see in the photograph. As a class, brainstorm other religious objects we use on holidays and Shabbat. *(ḥallah plate; ḥanukkiyah; seder plate)* Ask students to search with their family members for one or more Jewish objects in their homes (or something that could be used as a religious object; for example, a wine glass could be used as a Kiddush cup). Invite students to take a photograph or draw a picture of it and bring it to the next class. Explain that during the year students will learn about these and other ritual objects.

Page 7 **Talk About It:** Ask: Why might Elijah be sitting near these ancient scrolls? *(Answers may include: He wants to study them; Elijah lived a long time ago when there were no books and only scrolls.)* What scrolls do we still read from today? *(Torah; megillah)* If you could travel to ElijahRocks, what might you want to ask Elijah? *(Answers may include: Why do we build a sukkah? Why is it important to do mitzvot? What is the newest Jewish holiday?)*

Page 9 **Welcome to the Treasure Trail:** Ask: How many holidays will we learn about? *(twelve)* What will happen at each stop? *(A riddle will appear; students will solve the riddle.)*

Pages 10–11 **The Treasure Trail:** Acquaint students with the names of the Jewish holidays and the Hebrew months. Challenge them to locate various holidays or months on the Treasure Trail. For example, ask students to underline the month that sometimes has a second month *(Adar)*, to name the month whose name is only two letters long in both Hebrew and English *(Av)*, or to name three holidays that begin with the word "Yom" *(Yom Kippur; Yom Hashoah; Yom Ha'atzma'ut)*.

CHAPTER 2

ראשׁ הַשָּׁנָה

Rosh Hashanah

Textbook pages 12–23

Core Concept

On Rosh Hashanah, we celebrate the birthday of the world and the chance to make a fresh start for the new year.

Learning Objectives

Students will be able to:

- Explain the meaning of the four names of Rosh Hashanah.
- Identify the different shofar blasts.
- Discuss the role of the shofar in the celebration of Rosh Hashanah.
- Describe how we celebrate the birthday of the world.

Chapter Overview

At ElijahRocks, Daniel learns some other names for Rosh Hashanah and talks with Elijah about holiday customs, including dipping apples in honey, eating round ḥallah, sending greeting cards, and blowing the shofar.

Getting Started

Begin the class by asking: How do you like to celebrate your birthday? What was your favorite birthday celebration? Who did you celebrate with? *(Answers will vary.)* What do you need to have or do to celebrate a birthday? *(friends; family; special foods)* List students' responses to this last question on the board. Ask: How might we celebrate a birthday of our school? Our synagogue? Our town? Our world? *(special programs; meals; parades; parties)* Explain that, according to tradition, Rosh Hashanah is the birthday of the world. Tell students that in this chapter they are going to learn how people celebrate the birthday of the world.

Teaching Opportunities

Page 12

Hebrew Calendar: Direct students to the list of Hebrew months. Ask questions about the list, such as: How many Hebrew months are there? *(twelve)* What is the first month? *(Tishre)* What is the seventh month? *(Nisan)* You may wish to tell students that when there is a leap year in the Jewish calendar, there are two months of Adar—Adar I and Adar II. Ask students to circle and read aloud the month and date that are colored gold. (*Tishre 1*) Explain that the first of Tishre is always the Hebrew date for the first day of Rosh Hashanah.

Hebrew Month Song: Divide the class into groups of three to five students. Challenge groups to put the names of all the months to a song. Students might use a familiar tune, such as "Yankee Doodle," "Row, Row, Row Your Boat," or "Adon Olam," or create their own tune. Have each group present its Hebrew month song. Encourage all to join in. Consider singing one or two of the songs each time you study a holiday. Your students will know the Hebrew months in no time!

Photo Op: Ask: What is special about the *ḥallot* in this photograph? *(They are round.)* Why do you think we have round ḥallot on Rosh Hashanah? *(They look like birthday cakes; to be different from Shabbat; to remind us of the cycle of the year.)* Tell students that Jewish tradition has a number of explanations for why we use round ḥallot on Rosh Hashanah and that they will learn some of these reasons as they study this chapter (page 18 of the textbook).

Page 14

Hebrew Names: Encourage students to find out their Hebrew name and why they were given that name. Invite students to share stories of how their names were chosen. Check with your education director to see if there's a policy for how to proceed if a child does not have a Hebrew name. (For instance, the rabbi or education director might help the parents or family members choose a Hebrew name for the child.) Consider using your students' Hebrew names in class.

Put a Good Thought in Your *Rosh*: Ask the question in the textbook. *(Answers may include: help a friend with homework; teach a friend to play a new game; invite a friend over for dinner.)*

Page 15

Happy Birthday, World! Read aloud the text in the box and ask students to respond. *(Answers may include: my mom, because she reads to me; my dog, because he is fun to play with; camp, because I have lots of friends there.)*

Page 16

Photo Op: Call on a volunteer to describe Noah's birthday cake. As a class, share answers to the questions below the photograph. *(The cake might, for example, look like a forest, zoo, or globe; the world might wish for people to be peaceful, for there to be enough food for everyone, or for people to take care of the environment.)* Ask students what their own favorite cake might look like and why. *(Answers will vary.)*

Hands On: Draw an outline of a birthday cake on a large sheet of paper or poster board. Give each student a small construction-paper cutout of a candle. Have students write or draw a birthday wish for the world on their candles. Invite students to tape their candles onto the birthday cake and help decorate the cake.

Take a Vote: Write on the board: Which is harder, to apologize or to forgive? Direct students to close their eyes and put their heads down on their desks. Ask students who think it is harder to apologize to raise their hands. Next, ask those who think it is harder to forgive to raise their hands. Finally, ask who thinks that apologizing and forgiving are equally hard. Tally the numbers on the board and summarize the findings. Then, invite students to explain their responses and to give examples that show why it is harder to apologize or to forgive.

Page 17

Hands On: Prepare, or have each student prepare, a page that is divided into four quadrants, with one name of Rosh Hashanah in each section. *(Rosh Hashanah, Yom Hadin, Yom Hazikaron, Yom Teru'ah)* Ask students to draw a picture to represent each name. *(Possible illustrations include: the earth; a shofar; a person saying "I'm sorry;" a giant book.)*

Photo Op: Ask students to describe what the girl is doing in the photograph. Ask questions such as: Have you ever blown a shofar? If so, what was it like? How did you learn? When have you heard a shofar blown? What do you think of and how do you feel when you hear a shofar blast? *(Answers for the last question may include: excited that it is the holiday; reminds me to do good things; think of being in synagogue with my family and friends.)*

Blow the Shofar: Invite the cantor, rabbi, or another guest to blow a shofar for your students. Guide your students to call out the names of the blasts, and ask your guest to respond with those blasts. If possible, give students an opportunity to try out the shofar themselves. Use alcohol wipes to clean the mouthpiece after each student. After the visit, have students practice calling out the blasts and "singing" *(tu, tu, tu)* the sounds of the shofar or clapping the rhythm of the blasts.

Rosh Hashanah Vert Skate: If a computer is available in your school, allow students to play Rosh Hashanah Vert Skate at www.ElijahRocks.net. Consider having students take turns playing the game while others are completing another activity, such as creating Shanah Tovah cards (see suggestion for page 19). Encourage students to go to www.ElijahRocks.net on their home computer or on a library computer to play this Rosh Hashanah game. Encourage them to bring their score to the next class.

Page 18

***Tashlich* Invitation:** Discuss tashlich as a class. Encourage students who have gone to tashlich in the past to tell about their experience. Find out if your synagogue will be observing tashlich as a community. If so, have your students make an invitation for their families to come to tashlich. An invitation could read: Join us for tashlich on DATE at TIME at PLACE. Students can illustrate people throwing bread into the water.

Practice *Tashlich* in the Classroom: Spread a blue sheet or a slightly crumpled piece of blue mylar on the floor. Ask each student to write a bad habit or something he or she does that isn't nice *(such as teasing a sibling or tattling)* on a small piece of paper. Have students crumple their papers and throw them into the "stream." If they wish, they can talk about the habit or thing they want to get rid of.

Photo Op: Direct students' attention to the two photographs. Ask: What special items or foods do you see in these photographs? *(ceramic and silver Kiddush cups; two round ḥallot; honey)* When do you use special dishes or foods? *(when we have company; at a birthday party; on holidays)* How do you feel when you use these? *(excited; proud)*

Rosh Hashanah Blessings: Print and distribute the Rosh Hashanah blessings found at www.ElijahRocks.net. As a class, recite the Sheheḥeyanu and the blessings over the candles, wine, and ḥallah. If possible, bring candlesticks, candles, grape juice, and ḥallah to class. You might want to send a note to families suggesting that they visit www.ElijahRocks.net at home or at the library to get additional practice reciting these blessings. Recite the blessing over fruit and enjoy a snack of apples and honey. Or recite a modified version of the blessing that is traditionally said after eating apples and honey: "We hope that You, Adonai, renew for us a good and sweet year." Ask students what other foods they would use to represent the wish for a good and sweet year. *(chocolate bar; ice cream; pineapple)*

Page 19

New Year Wishes: Find out if there is a Jewish home in your area for older people or for people who are developmentally challenged. Give students construction paper, markers, glue, scissors, and old magazines to make Shanah Tovah greeting cards for residents of the home. You may wish to write frequently used words and phrases on the board to help students compose their New Year wishes.

The Name Game: From left to right, the holidays can match the cards as follows: The book is for *Yom Hadin* (the Day of Judgment, because God judges our behavior that is recorded in the Book of Life); the shofar is for *Yom Teru'ah* (the Day of the Sounding of the Shofar); the head is for Rosh Hashanah (the Head of the Year); and the calendar is for *Yom Hazikaron* (the Day of Remembering, because we remember our actions of the past year). Other answers may be given as well; for example, the head for Yom Hazikaron, because we think and remember with our minds; or the calendar for Rosh Hashanah, because the year can be recorded in a calendar. Be sure to ask students to explain their answers.

Photo Op: Ask: What symbols do you see on the New Year's card? *(apple slice dipped in honey; whole apple; pomegranate)* What symbols would you (or did you) draw on your Rosh Hashanah card? *(Answers will vary.)*

Pages 20–23

Rosh Hashanah Riddle: Write the Rosh Hashanah riddle from page 20 on the board. Ask students to guess what the answer might be. Write their guesses on the board. Read, or have students read, the story with a partner. Ask: What is the answer to the riddle? *(We answer the shofar's call when we admit that we have made mistakes, apologize, and try to do better.)*

Sticker Time: Invite students to look at the stickers in the back of the book, choose the one that best represents Rosh Hashanah (apple and honey), and place it in its spot on page 10.

Chapter Review

Rosh Hashanah Word Puzzle: Prepare copies of the Rosh Hashanah Word Puzzle found at www.ElijahRocks.net. Have students solve the puzzle with a partner. The answers are: HEAD; MAḤZOR; SHANAH TOVAH; TEKI'AH; YOM HADIN; HONEY.

Holiday Journal: Tell students that there are many different Rosh Hashanah customs. Explain that some families, for example, place a fish head on the table or eat a pomegranate. Have students write about or illustrate their favorite Rosh Hashanah custom. *(apples and honey; eating a fruit they haven't eaten for a year)*

Family Activity: Consider sending home a note explaining that the students have been learning about Rosh Hashanah customs, rituals, and values. Inform families that they can find Rosh Hashanah resources and games at www.ElijahRocks.net. Encourage families to make a list of things they can do for one another to help make the upcoming year good and sweet. Ask students to bring in their family lists to share with the class.

CHAPTER 3

יוֹם כִּפּוּר

Yom Kippur

Textbook pages 24–33

Core Concept

The Ten Days of Repentance that began with Rosh Hashanah end on Yom Kippur. On Yom Kippur, we ask God to forgive us for things we have done wrong, and we reflect on how to do better in the coming year.

Learning Objectives

Students will be able to:

- List the three steps to teshuvah.
- Describe the mitzvah of fasting on Yom Kippur.
- Explain the tradition of *yahrzeit*.
- Suggest several ways that people can give tzedakah.

Chapter Overview

At ElijahRocks, Rivkah learns about *tzedakah, teshuvah* (repentance), the custom of lighting a *yahrzeit* candle to remember loved ones who have died, and various prayers that are recited on Yom Kippur.

Getting Started

Call on volunteers to describe the picture on page 24. *(Observations may include: a white bag is hanging on the doorknob of a white door; the bag is decorated with a heart; the door is slightly ajar.)* Say: Imagine that the bag with the heart is holding "acts of loving-kindness." What kinds of actions might be in the bag? *(sticking up for a classmate; reading to a younger sibling)* How do you think you might benefit from doing these acts of loving-kindness? *(make a new friend; get along better with a sibling)* Explain that, in this chapter, students will learn how the customs and *mitzvot* of Yom Kippur can help us "open doors" to be our best.

Teaching Opportunities

Page 24

Hebrew Calendar: Point out the list of Hebrew months. Have students circle the month and date that are colored gold and invite them to chorally read the words. *(Tishre 10)* Tell students that the tenth of Tishre is always the Hebrew date for Yom Kippur. Ask: What is the Hebrew date of Rosh Hashanah? *(Tishre 1)* Explain that the ten days from Rosh Hashanah to Yom Kippur are very special and have their own name: the Ten Days of Repentance, or *Aseret Yemay Teshuvah*.

Hebrew Month Song: If your students created Hebrew month songs for Rosh Hashanah, invite a volunteer to lead the class in singing one of the songs.

Page 25

High Holy Days: Write on the board "Holy Days" and "Holidays." Explain that the word *holiday* is a combination of the words *holy* and *day*; tell students that *holiday* refers to a special day on which many people celebrate, remember an important event, and, in many cases, do not work. Have the class brainstorm a list of holidays, both secular and religious. On the board, add the word *High* to form the phrases "High Holy Days" and "High Holidays." Invite students to stand and reach up high. Ask: Do you ever place anything valuable or important up high? If so, why? *(a trophy from a competition, so it can be seen and won't get lost)* Why do you think we call Rosh Hashanah and Yom Kippur "High Holy Days" or "High Holidays"? *(Answers may include: because they bring us up high to God; because they are different from other holidays.)* Explain that the word *high* can also mean "important" and that these are the most important Jewish holidays, other than Shabbat.

Page 26

Three Steps to Teshuvah: Explain that *teshuvah* is the Hebrew word for repentance, which means to turn around, to change your ways. Have the students stand along the back wall of the classroom. Guide them to start walking toward the front of the room. Then, when you say "teshuvah," have the students repeat "teshuvah" together, turn around, and return to the back of the room. Then, have the students return to their seats. Ask: What does turning around and changing our ways have to do with the three steps to teshuvah listed on page 26? *(When we change our ways we apologize, we try to make up for the wrong, and we find a better way.)*

Photo Op: Ask students to imagine that the young girl in the photograph is about to apologize for something she has done. What are some things she might say to apologize? *(I'm sorry; I was wrong; I promise to behave better.)* What might she hope will happen after she apologizes? *(The person won't be angry; they will be friends again; the person won't feel hurt.)* Ask the questions in the photo caption. *(Answers may include: It's hard to admit when we are wrong; sometimes we're not sure how the other person will respond; we might feel better because the other person knows we regret the action and that we won't do it again.)*

Yom Kippur Blessings: Prepare and distribute copies of the Yom Kippur blessings found at www.ElijahRocks.net. Ask: Why don't we say Kiddush or Motzi on Yom Kippur? *(because it is a mitzvah to not eat on Yom Kippur)* Show students two candles and ask them to put a check next to the blessing recited when lighting candles. *(the first blessing)* Tell students that the second blessing, the Sheheḥeyanu, is said at the start of many Jewish holidays. Have students practice reciting both blessings. Send home a note to families inviting them to go to www.ElijahRocks.net and practice these blessings with their children.

Page 27

Night Time Is the Right Time to Begin: Explain that the beginning of Rosh Hashanah is called erev Rosh Hashanah. Remind students that Jewish holidays begin at sunset. Ask students to circle the picture that shows when Jewish holidays begin (the middle picture).

Fast Day: Remind students that it is considered a mitzvah to not eat on Yom Kippur. Ask: Who should not fast on Yom Kippur? *(young children; those who are ill; others for whom it would not be healthy to fast)* If you are too young to fast, but would like to, what might you do instead? *(not have an afternoon snack; avoid sweets during the holiday)* Guide children to understand that it is not healthy for them to fast, but there are healthy ways for them to make Yom Kippur special.

Page 28

Photo Op: Point out the *yahrzeit* candle in the photograph. Ask: What kinds of candles do you have in your home? *(birthday; Shabbat; Ḥanukkah)* Why do you think there is a special candle for remembering people we loved? *(because lighting the candle helps us remember them; because they were important to us)* Ask the question in the photo caption. *(Answers may include: because we shared the holidays with the people we loved; because these people made our holidays special.)* Point out the large black Hebrew letters in the photo, and tell students that the letters say *ner zikaron*, which means "memorial candle." Then, point to the small white Hebrew letters, and tell students that the letters say *ul'yom hakippurim*, which means "and for Yom Kippur," one of the days on which we light a memorial candle.

Kol Nidre: Ask: Do people always do what they say they're going to do? Consider sharing with students a time when you made a promise and didn't keep it. Ask: Have you ever made a promise you didn't keep? What was the promise? Why didn't you keep it? Allot time for students to share their experiences. Ask: What are some reasons we don't always keep our promises? *(We don't have time; we forget to do it; we have to do other things first.)* Direct students to read the last two paragraphs on page 28 and identify the prayer in which we ask God to forgive us for promises we could not keep. *(Kol Nidre)* Tell students that people refer to the erev Yom Kippur service as the Kol Nidre service.

Page 29

Photo Op: Call on a volunteer to read the caption next to the white Torah scrolls. Ask: Why do we dress the Torah scrolls in white on Yom Kippur? *(to remind us that the Torah teaches us how to live good lives; to remind us we can have a clean, fresh start to the year)* Tell students that on Yom Kippur many people wear white clothing and white *kippot*; explain that rabbis and cantors wear white robes. You may want to tell students that the Hebrew words on the lower left Torah mantle are *baḥodesh shofar*. Explain that these two words are part of the phrase *tiku baḥodesh shofar*, which is recited on Rosh Hashanah and means "Sound the shofar on the new moon." Read aloud the words on the lower right Torah mantle, *vayom hazeh yechapeir aleichem*—"On this day God will forgive you"; tell students that this is part of a phrase recited on Yom Kippur.

Photo Op: Point out the photograph of the bull's-eye, and ask students to identify what the children in the picture are doing. Draw three concentric circles on the board. In the outside circle write "Good," in the middle circle write "Better," and in the inner circle write "Best." Invite volunteers to stand three feet from the board and try to hit the "Best" circle with a small beanbag. Allow volunteers a few tries. Discuss how the exercise gets easier with practice. Explain that just as it gets easier to hit the mark when we practice throwing, it gets easier to do the right thing as we have more opportunities to try and practice doing the right thing.

Photo Op: Ask the questions in the photo caption at the bottom of the page. *(Answers may include: because I am a good friend; because I am nice to my sister; I might feel better about myself if rode my bike more often or if I read more books.)*

Page 30

Photo Op: Ask: What are the people in the photograph doing? *(filling a box with packaged foods)* Why do you think Yom Kippur is a time when many synagogues collect food for the needy? *(We are thinking about helping others; when we fast, we are reminded of others who are hungry.)* Tell students that it is a Jewish value to feed the hungry. If your synagogue is collecting food, take your students to the collection area to see how your congregation is helping others.

Tzedakah: Consider having your class participate in a tzedakah project that is organized by your synagogue. Your director should have access to a list of ongoing projects. Alternatively, if you have a tzedakah box in class, remind students to contribute. Tell students that later in the year your class will decide where to donate the tzedakah.

Page 31

Book of Jonah: Tell the story of the prophet Jonah (Jonah 1:1–4:11). You may wish to read the story from a children's version, such as *The Explorer's Bible, Volume 2* (Behrman House), Chapter 13; or check the synagogue or local library for other resources.

Yom Kippur Concentration: If there is a computer available, have students play Yom Kippur Concentration at www.ElijahRocks.net and match Yom Kippur words with their pictures. Encourage students to challenge their family members to a game using a computer at home or at the local library; have them bring in their score to the next class.

The Shofar's Call: Read aloud the text above the shofar. *(Responses may include: let my sister play with me and my friends; help clear dishes after dinner; walk the dog.)* Consider asking students to cut out a shofar shape from construction paper and write their resolutions on the shofar. With the students' permission, display the paper shofars on the classroom wall or bulletin board.

Pages 32–33

Yom Kippur Riddle: Read the riddle aloud to the class. In groups of three to four, have students read the text with the blue background on page 32. Ask: Why is the princess sad? *(She ran away from home; she did not think her parents would forgive her.)* How do you think the princess feels when she hears the messenger's words? *(happy because she would see her parents again)* What might be the answer to the Yom Kippur Riddle? Allow time for students to guess the answer; then have them read page 33 with their group. Again, ask for the answer to the riddle. *(teshuvah)* Discuss with students what teshuvah means. *(to return, to change your ways)*

Sticker Time: Ask students to choose the Yom Kippur sticker (shofar) from the back of the book and place it in the correct spot on page 10.

Chapter Review

Yom Kippur Word Puzzle: Prepare copies of the Yom Kippur Word Puzzle found at www.ElijahRocks.net. Have students work in pairs to solve the puzzle. Challenge student partners to locate all puzzle answer words in Chapter 3, such as teshuvah on page 26 and tzedakah on page 30. The first pair to complete the puzzle correctly and find all of the words is the winner. The answers to the puzzle are as follows: TESHUVAH; TZEDAKAH; KOL NIDRE; FAST; AL ḤET; YIZKOR; SHOFAR.

Holiday Journal: As a class, create a list of ways students can do better in the coming year. *(help my dad clean up the kitchen; eat healthful foods; recycle)* Invite students to draw a picture showing one thing they would like to do better. Encourage students to show their drawings to one another and describe their choices.

Family Activity: Consider sending a note home explaining that, while learning about Yom Kippur, the students discussed how feeding the hungry is a mitzvah. Encourage families to donate food to the needy. Provide a list of ways families can fulfill this mitzvah, including donating to MAZON (a national organization that works to alleviate hunger) and participating in the synagogue's food drive.

CHAPTER 4

סֻכּוֹת

Sukkot

Textbook pages 34–43

Core Concept

Sukkot, the autumn harvest festival, is a time of great joy. We say prayers of thanks to God and show our thanks by giving tzedakah to people in need.

Learning Objectives

Students will be able to:

- Name and describe each of the four species (the branches of the *lulav* and the *etrog*).
- Recognize three names for the holiday of Sukkot.
- Explain the biblical origin of Sukkot.
- Describe the properties of a sukkah.

Chapter Overview

At ElijahRocks, Daniel and Rivkah learn that it's a mitzvah to invite guests to eat with us in the sukkah; that we wave the *lulav* and *etrog*; and that our ancestors in ancient times slept in huts called *sukkot*.

Getting Started

Draw a picture of a sukkah on the board, or show students a photograph of a sukkah. Ask: Does anyone know what this is? *(sukkah)* How would you describe a sukkah? What do you know about a sukkah? *(looks like a hut; has branches on the roof)* What do you think it would be like to live in a sukkah? What might you like about it? What wouldn't you like about it? *(could be fun and different; you could see the moon and stars; would not be fun on a cold, wet night; might feel crowded)* Tell students that in this chapter they will learn about our ancestors who lived in these huts and about the *mitzvot* and customs of Sukkot.

Teaching Opportunities

Page 34

Hebrew Calendar: Point out the list of Hebrew months. Ask: What is the Hebrew date for Sukkot? *(Tishre 15)* Explain that there are twelve days between Rosh Hashanah and Sukkot, if you celebrate two days of Rosh Hashanah, or thirteen days, if you celebrate one day of Rosh Hashanah. Ask: How many days are between Yom Kippur and Sukkot? *(four)* Tell students that there is a tradition to begin building a sukkah right after the Yom Kippur break fast meal.

Hebrew Month Song: If your students created Hebrew month songs, invite a volunteer to lead the class in singing one of the songs.

Photo Op: Have students describe the photograph. Ask: Where do you think this sukkah might be? *(Chicago, Los Angeles, Jerusalem, or any place Jewish people live)* Help students understand that Jewish people everywhere build *sukkot* together on Sukkot. As a class, make decorations for the synagogue's sukkah. Students might, for example, create collages by cutting out designs from Rosh Hashanah cards and gluing them onto construction paper. If possible, laminate or cover the collage with contact paper. Many great ideas for creating sukkah decorations are available on the Internet.

Page 35

HANDS ON

Hands On: If possible, bring a *lulav* and *etrog* to class. (They should be available in your synagogue before and during Sukkot.) Divide the class into four groups. Give each group one of the four species (a branch of myrtle, palm, and willow, and an etrog), two sheets of paper, and a ruler. Ask students to write a description of their species on one paper and illustrate it on the other. On the board, write guiding questions such as: What is the length of your species? What is its width? What color is it? Does it have a smell? Assign group members specific jobs such as illustrator, recorder, investigator, and reporter. Have the reporter from each group report the group's findings to the class. (See the introduction for more about assigning jobs to group members.)

Page 36

A Picture-Perfect Sukkah: Ask: If Sukkot is seven days long and, according to Jewish tradition, we eat three meals a day in a sukkah, how many meals would we eat in a sukkah during the holiday? *(21)* Ask: Why do you think it is considered a mitzvah to invite guests to eat in your sukkah? *(because it's a nice thing to share food with friends; because it's good to invite people to your home, and a sukkah is like a small home)* Encourage students to share stories about having guests in their own sukkah, being a guest in someone else's sukkah, or eating a meal in the synagogue's sukkah.

Photo Op: Ask: What is the boy holding in his right hand? *(lulav)* What is he holding in his left hand? *(etrog)* Which direction is the tip of the etrog pointing? *(up)* Tell students that before we shake the lulav and etrog, we hold the etrog with the tip, *pitam*, down, and we recite the blessing over the lulav. We then turn the etrog so that the tip is pointing up.

Sukkot Blessings: Go to www.ElijahRocks.net and print out the blessings for Sukkot. As a class, practice saying the blessing that is recited before waving the lulav and etrog. Ask students to underline the words that are found in both blessings on this page as well as in the blessing before candle lighting (from *baruch*, "praised," through *vetzivanu*, "and commands us"). Explain that blessings said before performing a mitzvah begin with these words. Encourage students to practice these words at home with their family.

Hands On: Give each student a sheet of paper and ask the students to draw a picture of an etrog, including the pitam. Explain that the lulav and etrog are waved three times in six directions (east, south, west, north, upward, and downward) to remind us that God is everywhere. Have students pretend they are lulavs being waved. With your students, stand facing east, and hold an illustration of an etrog, with the pitam facing up. Step three times in the following directions: (1) forward then back; (2) to the right and back; (3) behind and back; (4) to the left and back; (5) go on tip-toe and back; and (6) bend knees and return to standing position. Encourage students to shake their shoulders so they are shaking like a lulav.

Page 37

Photo Op: Read the photograph caption aloud. Ask: Do you think it is warm or cold in Saint Petersburg, Russia, during Sukkot? *(probably cold because people are wearing winter jackets)* What languages are you most likely to hear in this sukkah? *(Russian, Hebrew)* Remind students that in Russia, and all over the world, Jews eat in a sukkah and recite blessings in Hebrew.

Concentration: Call on a volunteer to read aloud the second sentence in the second paragraph, telling how grapes, dates, and olives were harvested in ancient Israel in the autumn. Show students pictures of the seven species—olives, grapes, wheat, barley, pomegranates, dates, and figs—reviewing the name of each one. (Many images are available on the Internet.) Using two copies of each picture, play Concentration. Turn the pictures face down on a table. Divide the class into teams. Team members take turns turning over two pictures and naming the species. If the two cards match and the team can name the species correctly, the team takes the cards. If not, they turn the cards face down, and the other team takes a turn.

Hands On: To help your students better understand how long the Israelites wandered in the desert, write on the board: 40 years = 480 months = 2080 weeks = 14,610 days. Explain that the desert is very, very hot during the day and very cold at night. Invite a volunteer to role-play being an Israelite recounting the forty-year journey in the desert.

You're the Artist! Read aloud the You're the Artist! text. *(Responses may include: grandparents, friends, a favorite teacher; because I like them, because I miss them.)*

Page 38 **Photo Op:** Point to the photograph and read aloud the accompanying text. have students bring, grapes, dates, and different kinds of olives. Try to hav from Israel among the choices. For fun, have a taste test. Ask students to de of these three fruits they like best and least. For finicky eaters, ask them to which they think is the best looking.

An American-Style Sukkot: Read aloud An American-Style Sukkot. *(Respo include: recite a blessing over certain foods; decorate the table with gourds; pe mitzvah of* hachnasat orḥim *by inviting guests.)*

Talk About It: Read aloud the two paragraphs on the page. Ask: What two na Sukkot are found on page 38? What do these names mean? *(Zeman Simḥataynu—Time of Our Happiness; Ḥag Ha'asif—Harvest Festival)* Ask: If you were at the Temple in ancient times, what would you see and hear? *(see people coming from all over Israel carrying offerings; see people dancing; hear singing and instruments playing)*

Page 39 **A Festival on Foot:** Read aloud A Festival on Foot and allow time for students to fill in the names of the three pilgrimage holidays. *(Passover, Shavuot, and Sukkot)*

Photo Op: Point to the photograph and read the accompanying text aloud. Ask: Which blessing is the family reciting? *(candle lighting)* Use the blessings sheet from www.ElijahRocks.net and have students practice reciting the blessing for sitting in the sukkah.

Page 40 **Photo Op:** Ask students to read the photograph caption. Then ask: What are some other good and helpful things we can use our feet to carry us to? *(visiting an older relative; mailing a get-well card; bringing blankets to an animal shelter)* Consider having students trace outlines of their own feet, cut them out, and write their ideas on their paper feet. Display the feet on the wall or on a piece of poster board under the heading "Our Feet Carry Us Many Places."

Page 41 **Mayim:** Tell students that at the end of Sukkot, on Shemini Atzeret, we pray for rain to prepare the ground for planting. Tell students that *mayim* means water. Teach, or invite a guest to teach, your students to sing "Mayim" and to do a "mayim step." To do a mayim step, have students join hands and form a circle. Moving clockwise, (1) step right foot across in front of left foot, (2) step left with your left foot, (3) step right foot behind left foot, (4) step left with your left foot. Join your students in singing and dancing Mayim.

Sukkot Home Run Derby: If possible, have students go to www.ElijahRocks.net to play Sukkot Home Run Derby, matching Sukkot vocabulary and pictures. Encourage students to play the game with their families for fun and for additional review.

first two sentences in the box at the top of page 41 with the ts to look at the list of Hebrew months on page 34 and to ch as a raindrop or umbrella, next to each of the months from plain that in Israel it rains only during these months and not in Why do you think we say a prayer for rain on Shemini Atzeret? *d in a long time; because we need rain for crops to grow)*

students repeat the phrase *"ḥag samayaḥ"* after you. Guide all und the room and shake hands with each classmate as they wish *amayaḥ.*

Pages 42–43 Read the riddle aloud to the class. Have students read the story silently. Then, read the story aloud to the class. Invite volunteers to act out the story, or ask one student to be the "wise owl" and tell, in detail, how he or she saw each of the brothers put a portion of his harvest on his brother's pile. Ask: What might be the answer to the Sukkot riddle? *(tzedakah)*

Sticker Time: Ask students to choose the Sukkot sticker (lulav) from the back of the book and place it in the correct spot on page 10.

Chapter Review

True or False: Prepare a true and a false statement for each vocabulary word defined in the Sukkot Dictionary found at www.ElijahRocks.net—fourteen statements total. *(Examples: The branches on the top of the sukkah are called* lulavim *(plural of lulav). [False]; An etrog looks like a large, bumpy lemon. [True])* Give each student a copy of the vocabulary words. Divide the class into two teams, Team Alef and Team Bet. Have the teams take turns listening to you read a statement and then saying whether it is true or false. A team wins a point for each correct answer.

Sukkot Word Puzzle: Prepare copies of the Sukkot Word Puzzle found at www.ElijahRocks.net. Have students work in small groups to solve the puzzle. Challenge groups to write a new sentence for each of the answers. *(Example: We can make colorful decorations for the SUKKAH.)* Answers to the puzzle are as follows: HALLEL, TORAH, FRUITS, LULAV, ETROG, SUKKAH, MITZVAH, HARVEST.

Holiday Journal: Have each student write about or illustrate being in a sukkah. Encourage students to include details such as tables, chairs, decorations, the materials used for building the sukkah, and the people in the sukkah.

Family Activity: Encourage students to view images of *sukkot* on the Internet with their families and choose a picture of a sukkah they like. Students can draw a picture of the sukkah or print out the image and bring it to the next class to share with their classmates. Allot time for students to explain what they like about the sukkah.

CHAPTER 5

שִׂמְחַת תּוֹרָה

Simḥat Torah

Textbook pages 44–51

Core Concept

Simḥat Torah is a joyful time when we celebrate the gift of the Torah, which teaches us how to live as Jews and tells the stories of our ancestors.

Learning Objectives

Students will be able to:

- Describe how a Torah scroll is written.
- Explain that the Torah teaches us about *mitzvot* and tells stories about our people.
- Describe how we celebrate the Torah with singing, dancing, and *hakafot*.
- Recognize the English and Hebrew names of the books of the Torah.

Chapter Overview

At ElijahRocks, Daniel and Rivkah learn about the Torah. They learn how it is written, how it is dressed, the names of its books, and some of its well-known stories. They also learn how we celebrate when we complete a reading of the Torah and start the Torah anew—by singing, dancing, and parading with the Torah scrolls.

Getting Started

Ask: Do you have a favorite book that you have read more than once? A favorite movie that you have watched several times? Why do you reread a book or watch a movie for a second time? *(enjoy it; notice new things in it each time)* What book do Jews all over the world finish reading and then immediately start reading again every year? *(Torah)* Just like we see or learn new things each time we reread a favorite book or watch a favorite movie, we can learn many new things every year when we study Torah.

Teaching Opportunities

Page 44

Hebrew Calendar: Point out the list of Hebrew months. Ask students the Hebrew dates of Simḥat Torah. *(Tishre 22 and 23)* Tell students that many Jews celebrate Simḥat Torah on Tishre 23. Explain that in Israel and in many Reform and Reconstructionist congregations outside of Israel Simḥat Torah is celebrated, along with Shemini Atzeret, on Tishre 22.

Hebrew Month Song: If your students created Hebrew month songs, invite a volunteer to lead the class in singing one of the songs.

Photo Op: Call on volunteers to describe the photograph. Teach, or ask your cantor or music specialist to teach, the verse that is sung when we lift the Torah: *Ve'zot ha-Torah asher sam Moshe lifnei B'nei Yisra'el al pi Adonai b'yad Moshe.* Tell students that in English this means, "And this is the Torah that Moses placed before the people of Israel, by the word of Adonai through Moses."

Page 45

Ḥag Samayaḥ: Ask: How do we wish someone a happy holiday in Hebrew? *(ḥag samayaḥ)* What does *samayaḥ* mean? *(happy)* Which word in Simḥat Torah sounds a little like samayaḥ? *(Simḥat)* Tell students that Simḥat Torah means the happiness or joy of the Torah.

Page 46

Photo Op: Write on the board: Ths phtgrph shws sfr nd hs hlpr wrkng n trh scrll trh scrlls r wrttn n mny pcs f prchmnt (*Note: These are the consonants from the description in the photo caption.*) Challenge students to read what you have written. After a few students have tried to read it, ask students to read the photo caption. Explain that the Torah, like the sentences written on the board, has no vowels or punctuation. Tell students that to correctly read from the Torah, one must memorize all the vowels and punctuation. Explain that many Torah readers also learn how to chant each of the verses.

A Lot of Stories: Divide the class into three or four groups. Consider giving each group member a role, such as recorder, encourager, and reporter. Allow groups five minutes to create a list of stories from the Torah. At the end of five minutes, call on each group in turn to name one story from its list. List the stories on the board. As each story is named, instruct other groups to raise their hands if they have listed any of the same stories. If more than one group has listed a particular story, each of those groups should cross out the story from their lists. Continue until all groups have shared their full lists and crossed out any stories listed by another group. The group with the most stories remaining is the winner.

Unrolling the Scrolling: Read aloud Unrolling the Scrolling in the textbook and allow time for students to respond. *(Responses may include: Noah, Abraham, Sarah, Moses, and Miriam, or anyone who is mentioned in the Torah.)*

Mitzvot: Remind students that the Torah teaches us about *mitzvot*. Ask: What are some mitzvot we have discussed this year? *(hearing the shofar; sitting in a sukkah; welcoming guests; learning stories from the Torah)*

Page 47

Taste a Pomegranate: Bring a pomegranate to class for students to taste. Directions for easily and neatly cutting the fruit and removing its seeds can be found on the Internet. Remember to say the blessing over fruit. (You can find this blessing on the Rosh Hashanah blessings page at www.ElijahRocks.net.)

Photo Op: Have students look at the two photographs. Ask: How are the silver *rimonim* that decorate the Torah similar to the *rimon* (pomegranate) fruit? *(tops of the rimonim are shaped like pomegranates)* Tell students that some Torah scrolls are decorated with rimonim and others have a single crown. For fun, ask your students to guess how many Torah scrolls there are in your synagogue that have rimonim and how many have crowns. Record their guesses.

Hands On: Ask permission from your educational director or rabbi to bring your students to the sanctuary to view a Torah scroll up close. In the sanctuary, open the ark and count how many Torah scrolls have rimonim and how many have crowns. Compare the actual number to the students' guesses. Ask your educational director or rabbi to help you remove one Torah scroll from the ark. Undress it, lay it on the Torah scroll stand, and open it so students can view a few columns. Ask students to describe the Torah and how it is different from a regular book. *(It is all one long scroll, not pages; there are no vowels; there are no periods or commas.)* Point out to students that the Torah is written on pieces of parchment—made from animal skins—that have been sewn together.

Page 48

The Five Books of the Torah: Challenge students to learn the names of the books of the Torah in Hebrew and/or in English. *(The Hebrew names are B'reisheet, Sh'mot, Vayikra, B'midbar, D'varim.)* You might, for example, ask students to put the names of the books to a tune and have them practice singing the tune. Consider playing an echo game in which you say the Hebrew name and students respond with the matching English name. Alternatively, prepare ten game cards, each with one of the Hebrew or English names of the books of the Torah. Use these cards to play a memory matching game.

Photo Op: Call on a volunteer to describe the photograph and explain why it is an example of *tza'ar ba'alei ḥayim. (It is a kindness to provide water to a thirsty animal.)* Ask: How else can we perform the mitzvah of *tza'ar ba'alei ḥayim*? *(Donate blankets to an animal shelter; feed our pets; put out bird seed, especially in the winter.)* Tell students that the large Hebrew words on the stand mean, "drinking station," and the smaller words mean, "refresh yourself."

Page 49

Photo Op: Point to the photograph and ask: How many large blue Torah scrolls do you see in this photograph? *(four)* How many large white ones? *(one)* Explain that many synagogues have more than one Torah scroll and that on certain Shabbatot and holidays we read from two or even three scrolls. Challenge students to determine the total the number of Torah scrolls in your synagogue by adding the number with rimonim to the number with crowns.

Hands On: Remind students that we celebrate Simḥat Torah by singing and dancing. Teach, or invite the cantor or music specialist to teach, one or two songs that will be sung during your synagogue's *hakafot.*

Welcome to Talmud Torah! Read aloud the text in the box and allow time for students to respond. *(Responses may include: Rosh Hashanah has four names; we do teshuvah on Yom Kippur; it's a mitzvah to invite friends to eat in our sukkah.)*

Simḥat Torah Super Cart Race: If there is a computer available, invite students to go to www.ElijahRocks.net and play Simḥat Torah Super Cart Race. Students compete for the quickest time as they drive around a track and answer questions about Simḥat Torah. Encourage students to play the game with their families at home or at the public library. Challenge them to try to improve their racing time. Students might want to bring their scores to the next class to share with their classmates.

Page 50

Simḥat Torah Riddle: Read the riddle aloud to the class. Invite pairs of students to read the story together and raise their hands when they know the answer to the riddle. *(Torah)*

Act It Out: Invite two volunteers to come to the front of the room and act out the conversation between Hillel and the other man. Consider bringing two robes to class for the students to use as costumes.

The Whole Torah: Ask: Why do you think Hillel said that "Do not do to other people what you don't want them to do to you" is the whole Torah? *(because everything in the Torah teaches us to be nice to others; because the most important part of Torah is how we treat one another)* What are some ways we can follow Hillel's teaching? *(Do not tell bad things about another person; do not take something that belongs to another person.)*

Sticker Time: Ask students to choose the Simḥat Torah sticker (Torah scroll) from the back of the book and place it in the correct spot on page 10.

Chapter Review

Word Game: Before class, write the dictionary words from Rosh Hashanah, Yom Kippur, Sukkot, and Simḥat Torah on index cards—one word per card, leaving the other side blank. Turn the cards face down on a table. Divide the class into two teams, Team Alef and Team Bet. Invite a member of Team Alef to turn over a card, consult with his or her team, and give the meaning of the term. The team wins a point if the team member gives the correct definition. Teams take turns picking cards and defining the terms. The team with the most points wins.

Simḥat Torah Word Puzzle: Prepare copies of the Simḥat Torah Word Puzzle found at www.ElijahRocks.net. Have students work in pairs to solve the puzzle. Invite a student to illustrate one of the sentences on the board and to call on a classmate to identify the sentence. The student who correctly identifies the sentence goes to the board and illustrates another sentence. Answers to the puzzle are as follows: SCROLL, MITZVOT, HAKAFOT, GENESIS, ARON HAKODESH, SOFER.

Holiday Journal: Have students write about or illustrate their favorite story from the Torah.

Family Activity: Encourage families to read favorite stories from the Torah (children's versions) and/or watch a DVD of a story from the Torah. Check your synagogue library, local library, or Jewish community center for books and DVDs to recommend.

CHAPTER 6

שַׁבָּת

Shabbat

Textbook pages 52–63

Core Concept

Jewish tradition teaches that, just as God rested on the seventh day of Creation, people rest on Shabbat, the seventh day of the week. Shabbat is a day of joy, rest, and peace.

Learning Objectives

Students will be able to:

- Identify ritual items used on Shabbat.
- List traditions and *mitzvot* we perform on Shabbat.
- Explain the meaning of Shabbat Shalom.
- Describe the rituals that separate the end of Shabbat from the rest of the week.

Chapter Overview

At ElijahRocks, Daniel and Rivkah learn that Shabbat is a day of rest; it recalls the seventh day of Creation; we welcome Shabbat with candle lighting, Kiddush, and the Motzi; and we say good-bye to Shabbat with *havdalah.*

Getting Started

Write "Shabbat Shalom" on the board. Tell students that this is how we greet people on Shabbat. Explain that one of the meanings of *shalom* is peace, and that Shabbat is a day of joy, rest, and peace. Call on volunteers to describe peace. *(no fighting; quiet; people help one another)* Have students work in pairs to create a list of ways to make Shabbat peaceful. Invite students to share their lists with the class. Tell students that in this chapter they will learn about Shabbat and more ways to add shalom on Shabbat.

Teaching Opportunities

Page 52

Hebrew Calendar: Ask students how the list on this page is different from the lists on pages 12, 24, 34, and 44. *(This is a list of days, not months.)* Tell students that the Hebrew names for the days of the week are *Yom Rishon, Yom Sheini, Yom Shlishi, Yom R'vi'i, Yom Ḥamishi, Yom Shishi,* and *Shabbat.* Read aloud the Hebrew name for each day and have students repeat the name exactly as you say it. Ask students if they remember the meaning of the word *Yom. (day)* Explain that the first six days of the week are numbered, not named (First Day, Second Day, etc.). Explain that only the seventh day, Shabbat, is given a name.

Photo Op: Ask: How do you like to dress for special occasions? *(nice clothes; jewelry; dress shoes)* Point to the photograph. Ask: How is this table dressed for the special occasion of Shabbat? *(flowers; silver wine cup; candles; ḥallah cover; white tablecloth)* How do you think you would feel or what might you be thinking if you were sitting at this table? *(happy to be at such a pretty table; thinking about the good food that will be served)* Tell students that the words *Shabbat Shalom* are written on the ḥallah cover.

Page 53

Erev Shabbat: Ask students to circle the phrase "erev Shabbat." *(first paragraph, fourth line)* Refer students back to page 27. Ask: What is erev Yom Kippur? *(the evening or beginning of Yom Kippur)* What is erev Shabbat? *(the evening or beginning of Shabbat)* Does erev Shabbat fall on Thursday, Friday, or Saturday? *(Friday)* At what time of day? *(evening)* When does Shabbat begin? *(Friday evening, a little before nightfall)*

Page 54

Photo Op: Call on a volunteer to describe the photograph. Ask: What are some places where you would like to send tzedakah? *(Israel; food kitchen; animal shelter)* Ask the question in the photograph caption. *(Answers may include: It is a mitzvah to help others; we show that food and clothing belong to all of God's people.)*

HANDS ON

Hands On: Make tzedakah boxes with your students. Have students use a clean container from tennis balls, potato chips, or premade frostings. Students can cut out pictures from magazines that represent charitable organizations (e.g. clothing, food, animals) and glue these pictures onto the sides of the container. Encourage students to put tzedakah in their boxes at home each erev Shabbat.

Tell Students the Story of Creation. You may wish to read the account as told in *The Explorer's Bible Volume 1* (Behrman House), pages 8–13, or check the synagogue or local library for other resources.

Page 55

Shabbat Blessings: Give each student a copy of the Shabbat Blessings sheet found at www.ElijahRocks.net. Read and review each of the Friday night blessings (candle lighting, Kiddush, and Motzi). Have available candlesticks, a Kiddush cup, and a ḥallah cover. Display the objects one at a time, and have the class chorally recite the blessing that relates to each object.

A Holy Day: Ask students to find the word *holy* on page 55 and circle it. *(twice in the third line)* Write the following on the board: the Holy Temple; the Holy Ark; the High Holy Days. Ask: What word is in all of these names? *(Holy)* Ask: What else do we consider holy? *(Torah; siddur)* What do you think it means for something to be holy? *(special; different from everyday things; has to do with God)* What makes Shabbat holy? *(Shabbat is special; it is different from the other days of the week; it connects us to God.)*

Page 56

Photo Op: Point to the photograph and read aloud the caption. Tell students that there are different explanations for why we cover the ḥallah. Discuss how one tradition teaches that we cover the ḥallah so it won't be embarrassed when the candles and wine are blessed first. Ask: What does this tradition teach us about how to treat others? *(We must be careful not to embarrass others; we need to be considerate of other people's feelings.)*

Lecha Dodi: Read aloud the first three lines on the page. If possible, play the song "Lecha Dodi" in the classroom. Write *bride* near the top of the board. Ask students for words that describe a bride, and list their suggestions on the board. *(beautiful; wears white; happy)* Ask students to identify the words on the board that also describe Shabbat. Encourage students to use the words on the board to complete the following sentence: "Shabbat is like a bride because. . . "

Page 57

Shabbat Shalom: Teach, or ask your music specialist to teach, your students to sing "Shabbat Shalom."

Photo Op: Call on volunteers to describe the photograph. Tell students that the Hebrew word *yad,* which means hand, is also used to refer to the Torah pointer. Invite your students to point with their finger and pretend their hand, their *yad,* is a Torah pointer as they read the caption on this page. *(Answers to the question in the caption may include: We respect the Torah; we feel the Torah is very precious.)*

Page 58

You're the Artist! Read aloud the text in the box on page 58. *(Responses may include: play a board game with my sister; help set the table; clean my room.)*

Photo Op: Point out the photograph on page 58. Show the students a *havdalah* candle, a spice box, and a Kiddush cup. Your education director or rabbi should have these items available. Call on students to describe the havdalah candle. *(It has more than one wick; it is twisted; it is colorful.)* Pass the spice box for students to smell. Invite students to describe the smell and why they like it.

Havdalah Blessings: Give each student a copy of the Shabbat blessings from www.ElijahRocks.net. Practice reciting the four havdalah blessings: over wine or grape juice, over sweet spices, over the havdalah candle, and for separating Shabbat from the other days of the week.

Page 59

Eliyahu Hanavi: Teach, or ask your music specialist or cantor to teach, students to sing "Eliyahu Hanavi." (To hear this song, go to www.behrmanhouse.com and choose "Families," then "Celebrate Holidays," then "Passover." The words to the song are: *Eliyahu hanavi, Eliyahu haTishbi, Eliyahu, Eliyahu, Eliyahu haGil'adi. Bimheirah v'yameinu yavoh eileinu, im mashi'ach ben David, im mashi'ach ben David.*)

Hands On: Consider making havdalah part of your weekly class routine. According to Jewish tradition, havdalah can be done from the end of Shabbat through Tuesday afternoon. You will need a havdalah candle, grape juice, and a spice box. Each student might make a personal spice holder by placing a few cloves and a cinnamon stick in the center of a 4-inch square of netting, gathering the netting up over the spices, and tying the netting together with a piece of ribbon.

A Good Wish for the Week: Read aloud the text in the box. *(Responses may include: when I get to play with friends because I have fun with them; when I get a new game because it is exciting.)*

Page 60

It's a Match: Read aloud the instructions for It's a Match, and guide students to complete the activity. *(The pictures from left to right are: Kiddush cup, havdalah candle, ḥallah, Shabbat candles, spice box. We use a Kiddush cup at the beginning of Shabbat when we recite Kiddush and at end of Shabbat during havdalah.)*

Shabbat Slingshot: If a computer is available, have students go to www.ElijahRocks.net and play Shabbat Slingshot to review Shabbat and holiday objects.

Pages 61–63

Shabbat Riddle: Invite students to follow along as you read aloud the riddle and the Shabbat story. Ask students to underline the answer when it is read. *(the peace and delight of Shabbat)*

Shabbat Spice: Ask the class what they think Shabbat spice is made of. List their answers on the board. *(dinner with family and friends; time to play games and read books; meeting friends at synagogue)* Have students choose a favorite ingredient and explain their choice. *(For example: My favorite Shabbat ingredient is dinner because my whole family is together.)*

Sticker Time: Ask students to choose the Shabbat sticker (Kiddush cup and ḥallah) from the back of the book and place it in the correct spot on page 10.

Chapter Review

Tic-Tac-Toe: Give students a copy of the Shabbat Dictionary found at www.ElijahRocks.net. Divide the class into two teams, Alef and Bet. Allow team members five minutes to help one another learn the meaning of these words, and then collect the dictionary pages from them. Draw lines for tic-tac-toe on the board. Pick one of the Shabbat words and ask team Alef to define it. If the team members answer correctly, they write an X on the tic-tac-toe board. If not, the question goes to team Bet. Continue until one of the teams gets three marks in a row.

Shabbat Word Puzzle: Give pairs of students copies of the puzzle found at www.ElijahRocks.net and have them solve the puzzle. Challenge students to identify the sentences that describe an action over which we say a blessing. *(3, 4, and 5)* Answers to the puzzle are as follows: TZEDAKAH, FRIDAY, CANDLES, BRAIDED, CUP, SHALOM, HAVDALAH, KIDDUSH.

Holiday Journal: Have each student write about or draw a picture of something they can do to bring about Shabbat peace, Shabbat Shalom.

Family Activity: Encourage students to bring in favorite family recipes for chicken soup, noodle pudding, or other Shabbat foods. Collect the recipes to create a class Shabbat cookbook. Make copies and send the cookbook home with students.

CHAPTER 7

חֲנֻכָּה

Ḥanukkah

Textbook pages 64–75

Chapter Overview

Daniel looks forward to his favorite Ḥanukkah traditions, like playing dreidel, lighting the *ḥanukkiyah*, and eating latkes. At ElijahRocks, Daniel and Rivka learn how the Syrians ruled over Israel 2,000 years ago, and how Judah Maccabee and his men defeated the mighty Syrian army and restored the Temple.

Core Concept

The light of the Ḥanukkah candles reminds us of God's presence as we celebrate the miraculous victory of the Maccabees.

Getting Started

Ask: How do you feel after you win a game or competition? *(excited; relieved; proud)* How might you celebrate a big victory? *(party; meet with friends; have special food)* Tell students that each year on Ḥanukkah we celebrate a great victory. Explain that we are still proud of our victory 2,000 years ago when a small group of Jews overcame a very large, powerful army.

Learning Objectives

Students will be able to:

- **Name traditional Ḥanukkah foods and explain why we eat those foods.**
- **Tell the story of the Syrians desecrating the Temple and the Maccabees restoring it.**
- **Explain how to light a *ḥanukkiyah*.**
- **Play the dreidel game.**

Teaching Opportunities

Page 64

Hebrew Month Song: Call on a volunteer to identify the Hebrew date for Ḥanukkah. *(25th of Kislev)* If your students created Hebrew month songs, invite a volunteer to lead the class in singing one of the songs.

Photo Op: Ask: What night of Ḥanukkah is the family celebrating in the photograph? *(eighth)* How do you know? *(eight candles, plus the shamash)* What Ḥanukkah items do you see in the photograph? *(ḥanukkiyah; dreidels; coins to play dreidel; chocolate gelt* [gelt *is Yiddish for* money]) How else can we celebrate Ḥanukkah? *(have a party; invite family and friends for dinner; give one another presents)*

Page 65

Nes Gadol Hayah Sham: Have students practice saying the phrase "*nes gadol hayah sham*" several times. Ask them to stand and raise their hands high above their heads each time they say "gadol." Explain that the word *gadol* means great or big.

Hands On: Ask students to bring in a recipe for latkes. Have students compare the recipes, noting similarities and differences. Invite parents to help make latkes in class. Eat and enjoy the latkes with your students and guests.

Page 66

Photo Op: Ask students the questions from the caption. *(the fifth night; we can tell because there are six candles lit—a shamash and one for each of the five nights)* Ask students to describe the two *ḥanukkiyot* in the photograph. Tell students that many artists design ḥanukkiyot. Provide materials such as wood blocks, bolts for candleholders, glue, and paint for students to create their own ḥanukkiyot.

How to Light a Ḥanukkiyah: Challenge students to determine the number of candles needed to light the *ḥanukkiyah* all eight nights of Ḥanukkah. *(First night: 1 for the first night + 1 for the shamash = 2; second night: 2 + 1= 3; etc. Total: 2+3+4+5+6+7+8+9 = 44 candles)* You may want to have available a few boxes of candles to help reinforce the concept.

Play a Game of Po and Sham. Point to your feet, say "po," and motion for all students to come "here." Point to the other side of the room, say "sham," and motion for all students to go "there." Ask a volunteer to be the leader. Classmates move toward and away from the student leader as he or she calls out "po" and "sham."

Page 67

Light the *Ḥanukkiyah:* Read aloud the text and instructions on page 67. Guide students to draw the shamash in the middle and three candles on the right side. Have them draw the first flame over the shamash because we use the shamash to light other candles. Then have students draw flames on the candles in order from left to right.

Ḥanukkah Blessings: Copy and distribute the Ḥanukkah blessings page found at www.ElijahRocks.net. Teach students to sing the blessings. Send a note to families inviting them to visit www.ElijahRocks.net and practice these blessings with the children.

Page 68

What Do You Do? Read aloud the instructions in the What Do You Do box. *(Answers from left to right, top row: put in one; take everything; take half. Bottom row: get nothing; put in one. Students should circle the dreidel at the bottom right.)*

Playing Dreidel: Bring several dreidels to class. If possible, bring a dreidel from Israel. Invite students to compare the dreidels and discuss their similarities and differences. Have students play dreidel as part of a class Ḥanukkah celebration.

Photo Op: Ask students to identify the symbol on the Ḥanukkah gelt in the photograph. *(ḥanukkiyah)* Tell students that some gelt have the design of Israeli coins and some have a silhouette of Theodore Herzl, the man whose vision helped create the modern State of Israel. Ask: Why do you think these images appear on the chocolate gelt? *(They are important to Jews and Israel; they remind us that the Jewish people are strong.)*

Elijah's Dreidel-Click: If you have access to a computer, allow students to go to www.ElijahRocks.net and play Elijah's Dreidel-Click. Encourage students to play this game, and a real game of dreidel, at home with their family.

Pages 69–71

Hands On: Read the story of Ḥanukkah on pages 69–71. Divide the class into two teams. Give five index cards to each team and ask them to make up five questions based on the story. Teammates should write one question on each card, and the answer on the back of the card. Have teams take turns asking the other team questions. Award a point for every correct answer.

Pages 69–70

Talk About It: Ask: What did Antiochus forbid Jews to do? *(study Torah and celebrate Shabbat and Jewish holidays)* What did he order them to do? *(worship the Greek gods)* Why do you think he commanded them to do these things? *(so they would be like the Greeks; so they would forget their own history and traditions)*

Page 70

Seven-branch Menorah: Have students look at the menorahs on pages 69 and 70. Ask: What is different about them? Ask students to count the branches on the two menorahs. Explain that the menorah with seven branches on page 70 is an image of the menorah that stood in the Holy Temple. Explain that the ḥanukkiyah on page 69 has nine branches, one for each of the eight nights of Ḥanukkah, plus one for the shamash.

Page 71

Ḥag Ha'urim: Ask students to identify another name for Ḥanukkah. *(Ḥag Ha'urim, the Festival of Lights)* Challenge students to recall some other names for Rosh Hashanah and Sukkot. *(Rosh Hashanah—Yom Hazikaron, Yom Hadin, Yom Teru'ah; Sukkot—Zeman Simḥataynu, Ḥag Ha'asif)*

Page 72

Photo Op: Have students name the Ḥanukkah treats in the photographs. *(ḥanukkah gelt; potato latkes; jelly doughnuts—or sufganiyot in Hebrew)* Create a poster titled "Our Favorite Ḥanukkah Treats" and tally the number of students whose favorite Ḥanukkah treat is *sufganiyot*, Ḥanukkah gelt, or latkes. Have volunteers decorate the poster with illustrations of these foods.

Pages 73–75

Ḥanukkah Riddle: Ask students to read and guess the answer to the Ḥanukkah Riddle. *(the light of the ḥanukkiyah)* Have student partners read the story of the miracle of the oil. Ask: What does the light of the ḥanukkiyah remind us? *(that God is always present)*

Page 75

Add to the Light of Your Ḥanukkiyah: Read aloud the text in the box and ask students to answer the question. *(Answers may include: Give tzedakah; take care of pets; help a friend with homework.)*

Sticker Time: Ask students to choose the Ḥanukkah sticker (ḥanukkiyah) from the back of the book and place it in the correct spot on page 10.

Chapter Review

Word Pictures: Give each student a copy of the Ḥanukkah Dictionary words found at www.ElijahRocks.net. Write each word or phrase on a separate index card. Ask a volunteer to pick a card and illustrate the word or phrase on the board, without telling the class what it is. Call on students to guess the word or phrase being illustrated. The first student to correctly identify the picture gets to pick the next card.

Ḥanukkah Word Puzzle: Have student partners complete the puzzle found at www.ElijahRocks.net. Call on volunteers to write the answers on the board. Answers are as follows: IDOLS, MENORAH, PAY, MACCABEE, HAY, LATKES, EIGHTH, SHAMASH.

Holiday Journal: Have students write about or illustrate their favorite Ḥanukkah tradition. Encourage students to ask family members about their favorite Ḥanukkah tradition and share their responses in the next class.

Family Activity: Suggest that families investigate different organizations where they might donate tzedakah and encourage them to decide as a family to give tzedakah to one such organization. Your educational director or rabbi may be able to provide a list of recommended organizations to send home to families.

CHAPTER 8

ט״וּ בִּשְׁבָט

Tu BiShevat

Textbook pages 76–83

Chapter Overview

Rivkah and Daniel learn about a Tu BiShevat seder; the custom of eating fruits, especially the "seven species;" and Tu BiShevat *mitzvot* such as planting trees and caring for the environment.

Getting Started

As a class, list various "new years." *(January 1; the beginning of school; a birthday; Rosh Hashanah; the beginning of baseball season)* Remind students that we have already learned about Rosh Hashanah, the birthday of the world. Explain that now we will learn about another new year in Jewish tradition that celebrates the birthday, or new year, of the trees—Tu BiShevat.

Core Concept

On Tu BiShevat, the birthday, or new year, of the trees, we show our gratitude for all that trees provide, and we remember the importance of respecting and caring for the environment.

Learning Objectives

Students will be able to:

- Describe customs included in a Tu BiShevat seder.
- List benefits trees provide for people and animals.
- Explain how they can care for the environment.
- Tell why we recognize a birthday, or new year, of the trees.

Teaching Opportunities

Page 76

Hebrew Calendar: Call on a volunteer to read the gold-colored date. *(15th of Shevat)* Write *Tu BiShevat* on the board. Invite a student to circle the name of the month in which the holiday falls. *(Shevat)* Explain that Tu BiShevat means the 15th of Shevat.

Hebrew Month Song: If your students created Hebrew month songs, invite a volunteer to lead the class in singing one of the songs.

Photo Op: Ask students to identify the fruit in the photograph. Invite students to name some of their favorite fruits, and list these fruits on the board. Tell students that Judaism teaches us to value trees and the fruits that grow on them. Explain that trees are so important that Jewish tradition sets aside a special day marking the birthday, or new year, of the trees.

Page 77

B'seder: Ask: On what other holiday do we have a seder? *(Passover)* Explain that the word *seder* means order and that a seder is a meal that has a specific order. Write *b'seder* on the board. Tell students that in Hebrew, when you want to say that everything is okay, you say it is "in order," b'seder. Have students practice asking each other, "How are you?" and responding "b'seder." Consider including b'seder as part of your daily classroom vocabulary.

Page 78

A Birthday for Trees? Invite student partners to create a list of three to five rules for treating trees and plant life with respect. *(Don't pull branches off of a tree; don't pick wild flowers; water the plants in your garden.)* Read aloud the prompt at the bottom of the orange box and call on a student to respond. *(Rosh Hashanah)*

A Tu BiShevat Seder: Explain that we drink four kinds of wine or grape juice to remind us of the four seasons: White—winter; white mixed with a little red—spring; red mixed with a little white—summer; and red—fall. Challenge students to make up their own explanations for why we eat three different kinds of fruits. *(so we remember that all fruits are important; to show that even though things or people are different from one another, they are all important to us)*

HANDS ON

Hands On: If your school or synagogue is conducting a Tu BiShevat seder, have each student write and illustrate an invitation to bring home to his or her family. In addition to writing the time, date, and place on the invitation, students might want to include images of fruits and trees.

Birthday Wishes: Read aloud the prompt in blue at the bottom of page 78. *(Answers may include: I hope you get lots of sun; I hope you become tall and grow yummy fruit.)*

Page 79

True or False? Guide students to write T or F next to the statements in the textbook; then have them describe their favorite kind of tree. *(Answers: 1, 2, 3, 4, 5, and 7 are True; 6 and 8 are False. Possible answer: a maple tree because its leaves are colorful)* Divide the class into small groups. Consider giving each group member a role, such as recorder, encourager, and reporter. Provide support as the groups write four new true statements about trees. *(Examples: Some trees are good for climbing; many trees have pretty leaves; some trees live for hundreds of years.)* Invite each group's reporter to share its list with the class.

Photo Op: Read aloud the Hebrew for "Seven Species," *shiv'at haminim*. Have students chorally repeat the phrase. Call on seven volunteers to read the names of the seven species listed in the photo caption.

Hands On: Make collages of the seven species. Have available pictures of the seven species and products made from these foods. Pictures can be found in supermarket advertisements, magazines, and on the Internet. Have students sort the pictures by species, and assign each student (or pair or group of students) one of the seven species. Guide the students to make a collage with the pictures of their assigned species. Have each group present and describe its collage to the class. Display the seven collages on the bulletin board.

Page 80

Hands On: Tell students that the almond tree is one of the first trees to blossom in Israel, right around Tu BiShevat. Show students a picture of an almond tree in bloom and, if your school allows nuts to be served, serve whole almonds to your students. Be aware of any food allergies students may have.

Tu BiShevat Blessings: If your students are learning Hebrew, point out the word *Shevat* in the photograph of the platter (top left, on rim of platter) and the blessing over fruit (near the center of the platter, under the fruit basket). If possible, bring grape juice and dates or other fruits to class. Copy and distribute the page of Tu BiShevat blessings found at www.ElijahRocks.net. Join students in reciting the blessings before having the juice and fruit.

Letters That Count: Read aloud the text in the orange box. Write the letters and their number equivalent on the board. Then, invite students to make up equations using Hebrew letters. For example, *bet* + *gimmel* = *hay*.

Photo Op: If your students are learning Hebrew, ask for a volunteer to read the letters on the clock face. *(Clockwise from top right: alef, bet, gimel, dalet, hay, vav, zayin, het, tet, yud, yud alef, yud bet)* Read aloud the caption in the red circle and guide students to answer the question. *(Hay, the letter on the right at the bottom of the clock. It is positioned where 5 is normally placed.)*

Page 81

Photo Op: Read aloud the text in the blue caption and ask students to share answers to the questions. *(Answers may include: Trees also help animals by providing a home; they help all of us by providing healthy fruits.)* Consider showing students the children's food pyramid found on www.mypyramid.gov/kids. Ask students to describe how often they should eat fruit and how much fruit is recommended.

Photo Op: Ask the questions in the green caption. *(Answers may include: Recycling newspapers can help reduce the number of trees cut down for paper; riding a bicycle can cut down the amount of gasoline we use; riding a bicycle is also good exercise.)*

HANDS ON

Plant a Seed: Give each student a paper cup, soil, and a few parsley seeds. Have students plant the parsley seeds. Keep the cups by a window and have students water the parsley and watch it grow. Tell students that when Passover arrives they will have fresh parsley for their Passover seders.

Green List: As a class, create a "green list" of ways students can help take care of the environment. *(turning off lights when leaving a room; using a reusable lunch bag; writing on both sides of paper)* Consider having the class compose a letter to family members including this list and explaining how they hope to protect our resources.

ELIJAH ROCKS

Keep Israel Green: If a computer is available, have students go to www.ElijahRocks.net and play Keep Israel Green, fishing for items that come from trees. Suggest that students play the game with their families at home or at the public library and bring a list of the items they caught to the next class.

Pages 82–83

Tu BiShevat Riddle: Ask a volunteer to read the riddle aloud. Call on students to answer, and record their guesses on the board. Take students for a walk outside. Invite them to point out young, newly planted trees as well as older trees. Ask students to describe the differences between the younger and older trees. *(overall size, width of trunk)* Return to class and discuss how we enjoy the benefits of trees *(beauty, shade, fruits)* that were planted many years ago. Read to students the story of the carob tree on page 82. Discuss the importance of planting for the future. Ask students to find the answer to the riddle in the story. *(to plant trees and care for nature)*

Sticker Time: Ask students to choose the Tu BiShevat sticker (tree) from the back of the book and place it in the correct spot on page 10.

Chapter Review

Tu BiShevat Squares: Tell students that they will be playing a game like tic-tac-toe. Explain that in this game the game board is composed of nine students, one in each "square." You'll need ten sheets of construction paper, five each of two colors. Have three students sit on the floor, three more sit on chairs behind them, and three more stand behind them. Divide the rest of the class into two teams; for example, Blue Team and Red Team. A player on the Blue Team selects a square. Ask the student in that square a question about Tu BiShevat. The student gives an answer, and the Blue Team player must agree or disagree. If the Blue Team player is correct (agrees with a correct answer or disagrees with an incorrect answer), the student in that square displays a blue sheet of paper. Continue, alternating teams, until one team has three squares in a row.

Tu BiShevat Word Puzzle: Have student partners complete the puzzle found at www.ElijahRocks.net. Ask partners to choose one sentence and pantomime it for the class. Classmates can then guess which sentence is being presented. The answers to the Word Puzzle are as follows: FOUR, PLANT, FRUIT, SHEVAT, NEW YEAR, BLESSING, OLIVES.

Holiday Journal: Have students describe or illustrate in their journals a way they can take care of the environment.

Family Activity: Encourage students to take a walk in their neighborhood with a family member and locate two or three different kinds of trees. Suggest that they describe and note something special about each tree. Explain that, for example, they can sketch the tree and note that it has white bark, a wide trunk, and green leaves. If possible, they might collect leaves from the trees, and look on the Internet to identify the trees. Encourage students to bring their leaves to the next class and discuss their findings.

CHAPTER 9

פּוּרִים

Purim

Textbook pages 84–91

Core Concept

On Purim, we celebrate Queen Esther's courage when she spoke out against Haman's evil plan.

Learning Objectives

Students will be able to:

- Retell the story of Purim.
- Describe the mitzvot of *mishlo'aḥ manot* and giving to people in need.
- Give examples of how we can be like Esther and speak up against wrongdoing.
- Explain how Purim got its name.

Chapter Overview

Rivkah and Daniel discuss Purim traditions, including giving *mishlo'aḥ manot*, making noise with a gragger, dressing in costume, eating *hamantashen*, and hearing the story of Queen Esther from the *megillah*.

Getting Started

Ask: What are some things that make you happy? *(playing a fun game; spending time with my family)* Write on the board "Be Happy, It's Adar." Tell students that Purim is one of the happiest holidays of the year because long ago in Persia, now Iran, our people turned the terrible plans of our enemies upside down. Explain that, according to Jewish tradition, it is a mitzvah to be happy and to make others happy in the month of Adar.

Teaching Opportunities

Page 84

Hebrew Calendar: Call on a volunteer to read aloud the gold-colored Hebrew date. *(14th of Adar)* Tell students that during a leap year in the Hebrew calendar, there are two months of Adar—Adar I and Adar II. Explain that during a leap year, Purim is celebrated in Adar II. Consider having students look at a calendar to determine if it is currently a leap year.

Hebrew Month Song: If your students created Hebrew month songs, invite a volunteer to lead the class in singing one of the songs.

Photo Op: Point to the photograph. Ask: What are some clues that the people in the photograph are celebrating Purim? *(They are dressed in costume; they are smiling; a person is holding a noisemaker, or gragger.)* How can we tell that they are listening to the *megillah* reading, the story of Purim? *(People are holding books, probably to follow along with the reading.)* What do you enjoy most about Purim? Why? *(Answers will vary.)*

Page 85

HANDS ON

Hands On: Have students prepare *mishlo'aḥ manot* baskets. You might ask your educational director or rabbi to help you arrange to take the baskets to retirement homes or homes for people with disabilities. Consider having your class sing Purim songs when they deliver the baskets. You might want to have students make two baskets each—one to take home, and one to deliver to the group home.

HANDS ON

Hamantashen: For fun, bake *hamantashen* with the class. Have students experiment with novel fillings such as chocolate chips. Go to www.behrmanhouse.com/jam and click on "Purim" for a hamantashen recipe.

Page 86

HANDS ON

Photo Op: Invite students to suggest ideas for Purim costumes they might like. If possible, bring masks and costumes to class and have students dress up. Take photographs of the students to display on a "Be Happy, It's Adar" bulletin board. Alternatively, ask students to draw a self-portrait in a favorite costume. Ask the questions in the red photo caption. *(Answers may include: Queen Esther because she was brave; hamantashen because they are yummy.)*

Photo Op: Refer students back to page 57 in the textbook. Call on a volunteer to explain *sh'lom bayit. (peace in the home)* Ask: How can preparing mishlo'aḥ manot with your family add to sh'lom bayit? *(We all work together; we help one another; we have time to talk with one another.)* Turn back to page 86 and ask the question in the blue photo caption. *(Answers may include: raisins, grape juice, hamantashen.)*

Page 87

Photo Op: Point out the photograph and ask: What are some clues that this Purim celebration is in Israel? *(truck has Hebrew writing; Israeli flag)* How is this celebration different from our synagogue's Purim celebration? How is it similar? *(Answers will vary.)*

Pages 87–90

The Story of Purim: Ask students to follow along as you read aloud the story of Purim. Encourage students to stamp their feet each time they hear the name *Haman*.

Hands On: To create a class *megillah,* assign each student a sentence from the story that begins in the last paragraph on page 87. Distribute blank sheets of paper and ask students to copy the sentence onto the bottom of the paper and then illustrate it. Be sure all pages have a landscape orientation. Tape the pages together to create a megillah. Consider arranging the page order from right to left so it will read like a Hebrew megillah. Display the megillah on the bulletin board.

Page 88

Scrolling Along: Ask the educational director or rabbi if there is a megillah available to show to your students. If possible, open the megillah for students to view. Ask: How is this similar to a Torah? *(They are both handwritten; both are on parchment; both are scrolls, not pages.)* How is a megillah different from a Torah? *(A megillah has one roller, and a Torah has two; a megillah can be illustrated.)* Ask the question in the red photo caption. *(Answers may include: Mordecai standing in front of Haman, because he was brave; Esther speaking to the king, because she was brave and clever.)*

Page 89

Purim Word Search: If there is a computer available, challenge students to explain the significance of each word as they play Purim Word Search at www.ElijahRocks.net.

Photo Op: Point to the photograph and read the caption aloud. Ask: Why do you think it is a mitzvah to feed people who are hungry on Purim? *(Even when we are happy and celebrating, we need to remember to take care of people who are hungry.)*

It's a Mitzvah to Make Noise: Ask students to name the characters from the Purim story. *(Esther, Haman, Mordecai, Ahasuerus)* Invite students to decorate the gragger with a character from the story.

Page 90

Purim Riddle: Have student partners read aloud the Purim riddle and story on pages 90–91. Ask students to underline the answer to the riddle. *(speaking out with all your might)* Explain that there is a traditional Jewish value that teaches us to speak up, like Esther, when we see something wrong being done. Ask: Why is it sometimes hard to speak up against wrongdoing? *(We're afraid of what may happen; we don't want to get involved.)* Why is it important that we do speak up? *(to help make things right; to stop someone from hurting others; to show that we care)* Share a personal story about how you did or didn't speak up against a wrongdoing. Then, encourage students to share their stories.

Sticker Time: Ask students to choose the Purim sticker (Queen Esther) from the back of the book and place it in the correct spot on page 10.

Chapter Review

Haman Hangman: Play a game of "Haman Hangman." Choose a word or phrase from the Purim Dictionary found at www.ElijahRocks.net, or, if you choose, from any of the holiday dictionaries covered so far. You may want to distribute the dictionary page(s) to students. On the board, draw a "gallows" and a dash for each letter of the chosen word or phrase. Divide the class into two teams. Have teams take turns guessing the letters or the entire word or phrase. Fill in letters on the dashes each time a team guesses correctly. Add a body part to the "gallows" each time the letter chosen is not in the word. To win, a team must guess the word or phrase and say its meaning.

Purim Word Puzzle: Give students copies of the puzzle found at www.ElijahRocks.net. Divide the class into groups of three to four students. Have the groups complete the puzzle and then write the number of the page in the textbook where each answer can be found. *(pages 87; 85–86; 85–86 and 91; 87–90; 88; 89; 87–88 and 90–91)* The first group to correctly answer the questions and locate the answers is the winner. Answers are as follows: COSTUMES, HAMANTASHEN, MISHLO'AḤ MANOT, AHASUERUS, MEGILLAH, GRAGGER, ESTHER.

Holiday Journal: Have each student write about or illustrate a favorite Purim custom such as delivering mishlo'aḥ manot, dressing in costume, or hearing the megillah.

Family Activity: Tell families that one of the mitzvot of Purim is *seudat mitzvah*, having a festive meal. Encourage families to prepare and share a special meal together. You might suggest that they decorate the room with homemade Purim artwork. Families might add to the celebration by inviting a few friends or relatives to the dinner. Send a note home with students encouraging families to attend the synagogue Purim festivities (megillah reading and/or carnival).

CHAPTER 10

פֶּסַח

Passover

Textbook pages 92–103

Core Concept

On Passover, or *Pesaḥ* in Hebrew, we celebrate our liberation from slavery and remember the importance of freedom for us and for all people.

Learning Objectives

Students will be able to:

- Recite the Four Questions.
- Name and describe Passover ritual objects and the foods on the seder plate.
- Explain why we do not eat ḥametz during Passover.
- Retell the story of our exodus from Egypt.

Chapter Overview

Daniel's family cleans out all the ḥametz to prepare for Passover. At ElijahRocks, Daniel, Rivkah, and Elijah tell the story of the Israelites being freed from slavery in Egypt. We retell this story at the Passover seder using the haggadah, ritual objects such as the seder plate and Elijah's Cup, and special foods like *ḥaroset* and matzah.

Getting Started

Ask students to think of a time when they had to rush to get somewhere. Ask: What did you do? How did it feel to have to rush? Did you forget anything? *(Answers may include: I was late for a soccer game; I almost missed the school bus; it was not easy to rush; it was upsetting. I forgot my folder; I forgot to have breakfast.)* Tell students that in this chapter they will learn the story of Passover and will hear about the Israelites, who left Egypt in a big hurry long ago.

Teaching Opportunities

Page 92

Hebrew Calendar: Call on a volunteer to read the gold-colored Hebrew date. *(15th of Nisan)* Encourage students to look for the moon the night the holiday begins. What phase is the moon? *(full moon)* Tell students that the Hebrew calendar follows the phases of the moon; so there is always a full moon in the middle of each month. Ask: Why would this be a good time of month for the Israelites to leave Egypt? *(The strong light of the full moon would help them to see when traveling at night.)*

Hebrew Month Song: If your students created Hebrew month songs, invite a volunteer to lead the class in singing one of the songs.

Photo Op: Call on volunteers to describe the objects in the photograph that are connected to mitzvot. *(haggadah; wine; candles)* Inform students that *hiddur mitzvah*, making a mitzvah beautiful, is a traditional Jewish value. Ask: How is this seder table an example of hiddur mitzvah? *(nice dishes and glasses; flowers; tablecloth)* Can you think of other examples of hiddur mitzvah? *(a pretty ḥanukkiyah; a colorful ḥallah cover; a special mezuzah)* What might you put on your seder table to carry out hiddur mitzvah? *(Answers will vary.)*

Page 93

HANDS ON

Hands On: Have students search for ḥametz in your classroom. You will need a wooden spoon, a feather, a candle, and a bag. Hide pieces of bread for students to find. Consider having students bring in flashlights to look for the ḥametz. Have students use the feather to sweep the ḥametz onto the spoon and then drop the ḥametz into the bag. Complete directions for performing *bedikat ḥametz*, "inspection for leavened food," can be found in some *haggadot* and on the Internet.

Page 94

Photo Op: Point to the photograph and read aloud the caption in the blue circle. Give each student a sheet of construction paper. Have students fold the paper into four equal rectangles and draw the outline of a wine cup in each quadrant. Guide students to decorate the wine cups with symbols and words related to each of the four promises.

Why Matzah? Ask students why we eat matzah on Passover. Record students' answers on the board. Then, encourage student partners to check their answers by reading the two paragraphs in the box.

Page 95

Afikoman: Read aloud the text in the box and invite students to share and explain their families' best hiding places. *(under the couch because it is dark; inside a kitchen drawer because it is completely hidden)* Take a class survey and tally how many students attend seders in which children hide the afikoman and how many attend seders in which the adults hide it.

The Four Questions: Distribute copies of the Four Questions found at www.ElijahRocks.net and have the class take turns reading the questions aloud in English. Teach, or have your cantor or music specialist teach, students to chant the Four Questions in Hebrew. Explain that the youngest child at the seder traditionally asks the Four Questions. Send a note to families inviting them to go to www.ElijahRocks.net and practice with their child.

Page 96

Photo Op: Call on students to describe the photograph of the seder. Ask a volunteer to tell how this seder looks similar to one he or she may have attended. *(There is a seder plate; people are singing or saying a blessing.)* How does it look different? *(There is matzah on the seder plate; there are more/fewer people.)* Explain that different families have different customs. For instance, there is a Persian custom of participants lightly hitting one another with scallions, as if they were taskmasters' whips, while singing "Dayeinu." Encourage students to share their favorite family seder traditions.

The Story of Passover: Have students take turns reading aloud paragraphs of the story from the middle of page 96 to page 99. Ask students to reread the last paragraph on page 96 and identify the three women or girls who together saved the baby Moses. *(his mother; his sister; Pharoah's daughter)* Ask: Who do you think was bravest? Why? What questions would you want to ask any of these women? Why? *(Answers will vary.)*

Page 97

The Ten Plagues: Before class, prepare a list of ten made-up "plagues" that are not in the Passover story. For example, "All the land flooded" or "the Nile River dried up." As a class, read aloud the ten plagues. Divide the class into two teams, Alef and Bet. Read either a plague you invented or a plague described on page 97. Teams Alef and Bet take turns saying if the plague is part of the Passover story or not. The team with the most points is the winner.

Page 98

The Seder Plate: Ask: What special foods do we eat on other Jewish holidays? What do these foods remind us of? *(On Rosh Hashanah, we eat apples with honey for a sweet year; on Ḥanukkah, we eat latkes to remember the legend of the oil.)* Tell students that just like we do on other Jewish holidays, on Pesaḥ we eat special foods that serve as reminders. Have students read and complete page 98. *(Sample answer for last question: a carrot, because carrots are hard, and the Israelites worked hard.)* Give each student a sheet of paper to illustrate the food they might want to add to the seder plate. Encourage students to write a sentence explaining their choice. Display the drawings in the classroom.

Hands On: Invite students to bring in a family recipe for ḥaroset. Alternatively, bring in a variety of ḥaroset recipes from newspapers, magazines, cookbooks, or the internet. Compile a ḥaroset recipe page to send home to families. Consider making some of the recipes in class and having a ḥaroset tasting party. Don't forget the matzah to eat it with! Be sure to check first if your school has a policy about serving nuts, or a policy about serving matzah before Passover.

Passover Blessings: Distribute the Passover blessings page found at www.ElijahRocks.net. As a class, practice the blessings said at the Passover seder. Challenge students to find photographs in Chapter 10 for the foods over which these blessings are said. *(fruit of the vine—page 92; fruit of the earth, bitter herbs—page 98; bread from the earth, matzah—page 95)* Send a note home inviting families to go to www.ElijahRocks.net to practice these blessings.

Seder Plate Simon: If possible, have students go to www.ElijahRocks.net and play Seder Plate Simon to reinforce Passover vocabulary and pictures. Encourage students to play the game with their families for fun and for additional review.

Page 99

Passed Over: Challenge students to find and circle the words in the first paragraph on page 99 from which Passover gets its name. *(passed over)* Ask: What was passed over? *(the homes of the Israelites)* Explain that according to the Torah God was able to identify the homes of our ancestors, the Israelites. What are some ways that a visitor might be able to tell that you live in a Jewish home? *(mezuzah; ḥanukkiyah; seder plate; books written in Hebrew)*

Point of View: Write the following questions on the board: How do you feel as the Israelites are leaving Egypt? What are you afraid of? What are you hoping for? Divide the class into three groups: Moses, Pharoah, and the Israelites. Consider giving each group member a role, such as recorder, encourager, and reporter. Guide each group to discuss the questions based on their character, and then share the character's responses with the class. Tell students that Jewish tradition teaches that we must imagine ourselves as if we were personally freed from Egypt.

Sense Something Special? Read aloud the text in the box on page 99 and guide students to complete the exercise. *(Responses may include: See—seder plate, haggadah; Hear—Four Questions, Pesaḥ songs; Touch—matzah, wine glass; Taste—ḥaroset, maror; Smell—candles, grape juice, matzah ball soup.)*

Pages 100–101 **Passover Riddle:** Divide the class into small groups. Have each group read the riddle and write down possible answers. Ask a representative from each group to share its answers. Record the guesses on the board. Ask the groups to read pages 100–101 and raise hands when they find the answer to the riddle. *(worship God, which includes helping others)*

Page 101 **Feed People Who Are Hungry:** Tell students that Jewish tradition teaches us that feeding people who are hungry, *ma'achil r'eivim*, is our responsibility. If your synagogue has a food drive, encourage students to bring nonperishable, kosher-for-Passover foods to the synagogue. Alternatively, if you collect tzedakah in your class, get students' permission to send the class tzedakah to a charitable organization, such as MAZON, that supports food banks.

Free the Captive: Inspire your students with modern day accounts of *pidyon sh'vuim*, redeeming captives. Tell how the Jewish community has upheld this value by bringing thousands of Jews out of countries such as the former Soviet Union and Ethiopia so they could live freely as Jews. You can find details about these historic events in *The History of the Jewish People, Volume 2* (Behrman House), chapters 11–12; or check your local or synagogue library for other resources.

Page 102 **Elijah's Cup:** Sing "Eliyahu Hanavi" with the class. Ask students on what other day we traditionally sing this song. (*Shabbat; see textbook page 59.*) Explain that by welcoming the prophet Elijah to our seder with an open door and a special cup of wine we are inviting peace to come into the world.

Miriam's Cup: Ask students to read the second paragraph on page 102. Ask: Why do some families have a Cup of Miriam, and why is it filled with water? *(to honor Miriam's courage and inspiration; Miriam's well gave the Israelites water in the desert; Miriam watched over baby Moses in the Nile River.)*

Page 103 **Photo Op:** Point to the photograph and ask the question in the caption. *(Responses may include: We need to care about all people; all human life is important; we should not be joyful over another person's suffering.)*

For Fun: Take a survey: How many of your students take the drops out of the cup with a spoon? How many take them out with a finger? Explain that this is an example of a tradition that can be carried out in different ways.

Sticker Time: Ask students to choose the Passover sticker (seder plate) from the back of the book and place it in the correct spot on page 11.

Chapter Review

Word Game: Distribute copies of the Passover Dictionary found at www.ElijahRocks.net. Divide the class into two teams, Alef and Bet. Ask team Alef a question based on the Passover Dictionary. Sample questions include: What is usually recited by the youngest child? *(Four Questions)* What do we call the piece of matzah broken in half during the seder? *(Afikoman)* If team Alef answers correctly, the team writes one of the letters from the word *Passover* on the board. Teams take turns answering questions and adding a letter for each correct answer. The first team to spell *Passover* is the winner.

Passover Word Puzzle: Give each student a copy of the Passover Word Puzzle found at www.ElijahRocks.net. Have student partners complete the puzzle. Challenge students to search in the answer words and circle the letters that spell the name of the prophet who led the Israelites out of Egypt. *(Moses)* Answers to the puzzle are as follows: PESAḤ, MATZAH, FOUR, MAROR, PASSOVER, ELIJAH'S, SALT, ḤAROSET.

Holiday Journal: Have students write about or illustrate their favorite part of the seder. Students might, for example, journal about reciting the Four Questions, finding the afikoman, eating macaroons, or hearing the Passover story.

Family Activity: Send a note home inviting families to have a seder at home. Encourage families to prepare activities and props in advance of the seder. Suggestions include gathering items such as plastic insects and toy frogs to represent the plagues; making seder plates or matzah covers; and teaching children songs such as "Dayenu" so they can sing along at the seder. Encourage families to have fun and use their imaginations to liven up the seder.

CHAPTER 11

יוֹם הַשּׁוֹאָה

Yom Hashoah

Textbook pages 104–107

Core Concept

The Holocaust underscores the importance of acceptance and respect for others—even those who are different from us—and the obligation to speak up in the face of injustice.

Learning Objectives

Students will be able to:

- Give examples of speaking up against injustices.
- Explain the importance of acceptance and respect for others.
- Discuss how we can learn from our experiences.
- Tell how Yom Hashoah memorializes Jews who lost their lives during the Holocaust.

Chapter Overview

On Yom Hashoah, Holocaust Memorial Day, we remember the millions of people who died during the Holocaust. On Yom Hashoah, we have special prayer services and light a memorial candle in memory of those who died.

Special Note: It is essential to remember that when teaching about Yom Hashoah to second and third graders, we do not tell the atrocities of the Holocaust. This information can be quite traumatizing. Rather, it is our obligation to teach young children to accept and respect others—including those who are different from us—and to have the courage to speak out against a wrong.

You might want to send a letter home to families in advance of the lesson informing them that the children will be learning about Yom Hashoah. Let family members know that this year's study of the Holocaust will focus on the importance of acceptance and respect for others, and of speaking out against unfair treatment of others. At an older age, students will be introduced to the events of the Holocaust.

Getting Started

Tell students that unlike most of the special days on the Jewish calendar, Yom Hashoah, Holocaust Memorial Day, is a sad day. Explain that you are aware that some of them may know more than others about the events of the Holocaust, but that in class you will not be discussing the events of the Holocaust. Rather, you will be discussing how Yom Hashoah reminds us to treat all people fairly and to respect others even if they are different from us. In advance of the lesson, you might consider checking out age-appropriate books about the Holocaust from the local library or synagogue library so you will be prepared to answer students' specific questions. You might also consider inviting your rabbi to attend the first part of this class so he or she can answer students' questions.

Teaching Opportunities

Page 104 **Hebrew Calendar:** Tell students that this chapter is devoted to a very sad day on the Jewish calendar, Nisan 27. Explain that because this is a sad day and you wish to keep the mood serious, if your class has been singing the Hebrew month songs, they will not do this today.

Page 104 **Photo Op:** Call on volunteers to describe the sculpture in the photograph. *(There is a Jewish star, magen David, outlined by the sculpture; there is a pointed column in the middle of the sculpture; the sculpture is outdoors.)* Tell students that this sculpture is called The Memorial to the Jewish Soldiers and Partisans. Explain that the sculpture is in Israel and it is dedicated to the memory of the many brave Jews who lost their lives as they fought against Adolf Hitler. Tell students that when we see this sculpture we remember their courage and bravery.

Page 105 **Learning From Experience:** Write the following sentence on the board: "We learn from experience." Call on volunteers to explain what it means. Share an example of how you learned from an experience, and then invite students to share their examples of learning from an experience. Students may, for example, have learned not to hurt another person's feelings after having their own feelings hurt. Or, they may have learned to help others and to be patient after having someone patiently help them with homework. Explain that even though Yom Hashoah is a very sad day, it is important for us to remember this day and to learn from our history.

Respect and Acceptance: Consider reading or showing a DVD of a story about respect and acceptance. *The Sneetches* by Dr. Seuss, for example, offers students opportunities to learn about the value of accepting and respecting people who are different.

Page 106

Memorial Candle: Ask: On what holiday do we light a candle to remind us of people we loved who have died? *(Yom Kippur)* Tell students that on Yom Hashoah we light a memorial candle to remember the Jews who lost their lives during the Holocaust. Explain that this candle can also remind us of the kind of world we hope for. Write on the board: "On Yom Hashoah we light a memorial candle and we hope that _____." Invite students to share their hopes for the world. Ask students to write their hopes on construction paper candles to display in the classroom.

Page 107

Talk About It: Ask students the question about bullying on page 107. *(Answers may include: Tell the bully to stop; tell a teacher or other trusted adult; be kind to the person being bullied.)*

Sticker Time: Ask students to choose the Yom Hashoah sticker (*yahrzeit* candle) from the back of the book and place it in the correct spot on page 11.

Chapter Review

Holiday Journal: Invite students to write about or draw a picture illustrating that it is important to respect people—even people who are different from us, to treat them fairly, and to speak up against injustice. Encourage students to share their writings or illustrations with classmates.

Family Activity: Send a note home to families to ask if anyone in their family is or was a Holocaust survivor, or a soldier who fought in World War II. Encourage survivors to talk to the children about their experiences and about the lessons of acceptance and respect for others.

CHAPTER 12

יוֹם הָעַצְמָאוּת

Yom Ha'atzma'ut

Textbook pages 108–117

Chapter Overview

Rivkah and Daniel discuss how Israel became an independent Jewish state after almost 2000 years of foreign rule, and how Yom Ha'atzma'ut, Israeli Independence Day, is celebrated today both in Israel and in North America.

Core Concept

Israel is the homeland of the Jewish people, a country that welcomes Jews from around the world.

Getting Started

Write on the board "Happy Birthday Israel." Invite students to join with you in singing "Happy Birthday to You" or *Yom Huledet Sameaḥ* (to the same tune) to Israel. Challenge students to calculate the age of the State of Israel. Invite a volunteer to write an equation on the board: (The current year) – 1948 = (Israel's age). As a class, brainstorm a list of birthday wishes for Israel.

Learning Objectives

Students will be able to:

- **Tell some of the steps that led to the creation of the State of Israel.**
- **Describe how Yom Ha'atzma'ut is celebrated in Israel and in North America.**
- **Identify the Israeli flag.**
- **Recognize "Hatikvah" as the Israeli national anthem.**

Teaching Opportunities

Page 108

Hebrew Month Song: Call on a volunteer to read the date *(5th of Iyar).* If your students created Hebrew month songs, invite a volunteer to lead the class in singing one of the songs.

Photo Op: Point to the photograph. Ask: What images are on the props the marchers are carrying? *(Torah; map of Israel; Israeli flag)* Why do you think the marchers chose these symbols? *(The flag reminds us that we have a Jewish country; Torah is important for all Jews; the smiling map reminds us of our love for Israel.)* Tell students that the hats drawn on the illustrated characters are often referred to as "kibbutz hats." Explain that these hats were very popular when Israel first became a state.

Page 109

Say Yom Ha'atzma'ut: Ask students to chorally repeat the name of the holiday: Yom Ha'atzma'ut. Consider having students pass around a small Israeli flag as they say the holiday's name. Challenge the students to see how fast they can each correctly say, "Yom Ha'atzma'ut." Ask students to review the first paragraph and infer the meaning of the word *atzma'ut. (Independence)*

Independence Days: Draw a line down a sheet of poster board to create two columns. Label one column "Yom Ha'atzma'ut" and the other "Fourth of July" (or "Canada Day"). As you read the chapter, have students list comparisons between the two days. Discuss the similarities and differences. *(Responses for Yom Ha'atzma'ut may include: Independence Day in Israel; Iyar 5 in the Hebrew calendar; 1948; parades, fireworks, picnics; Jews around the world celebrate. Responses for the Fourth of July may include: Independence Day in the United States; July 4 in the Gregorian calendar; 1776; parades, fireworks, picnics; U.S. residents celebrate.)*

Page 110

Hands On: Tell students that a decoration called a *mizraḥ*, meaning east, hangs on an eastern wall in many Jewish homes and synagogues to remind us that Jerusalem is to the east. Bring in, or encourage students to bring in, pictures of Jerusalem from magazines, newspapers, or the Internet. Write MIZRAḤ on a large sheet of poster board. As a class, mount the images of Jerusalem on the poster board to create a mizraḥ collage. Hang the mizraḥ on the eastern wall of your classroom.

Talk About It: Ask: What makes the state we live in different from the state next to ours? *(different leaders; different rules)* What does the word *land* make you think of? *(the ground; the place we live)* Write on the board: "Land of Israel" and "State of Israel." Ask: What makes a state different than a land? *(A state has its own government; a land is where people live.)* What is the difference between the two phrases on the board? *(The Land of Israel has been home to Jews for thousands of years, but the State of Israel, the modern nation under a Jewish government, came into existence in 1948.)*

Photo Op: Point to the photograph and read aloud the caption. Ask: What would you think if you saw a camel on the sidewalk? What two types of transportation are shown in this photo? *(camel; cars)* Point out that in this photograph we see an example of how the ancient and the modern worlds coexist in Israel today.

Page 111 **Rebuilding the Land:** Read aloud the text in the orange box. Ask: If you were a pioneer moving to Eretz Yisrael, would you choose to live on a kibbutz or in a city? Why?

You're the Artist! Read aloud You're the Artist! and prompt students to take time illustrating their life in Israel. *(Possible captions include: It is exciting to be rebuilding Jerusalem; I am working hard, but I feel like I'm home.)*

Page 112 **Going Up:** Read aloud the text in the box. *(Responses may include: both bring us closer to God; we have to go up steps to go to a bimah; both bring us to an important, holy place.)*

Hatikvah: Ask students how hoping for something can help us to reach our dreams. *(It may make us work harder to get it.)* Explain that *Hatikvah* means "The Hope" in Hebrew, and that Israel's national anthem expresses the hope that Jews will live as free people in Eretz Yisrael. Teach students "Hatikvah," or have your music specialist or cantor teach the song. The words and music can be found at www.ElijahRocks.net.

Page 113 **Photo Op:** Point out that the students in the photograph are learning about Israel by looking at a map. Ask: What are other ways we can learn about Israel? *(magazines; Internet; television; newspapers; visiting)* Read aloud the caption and ask students to share what they know about Israel. Consider recording students' knowledge on the board. *(Answers may include: people speak Hebrew in Israel; Abraham lived in the land of Israel.)*

Why? What? Where? Read aloud the text in the box and prompt students to share their questions about Israel. *(Questions may include: Why do Israelis speak Hebrew? What sports teams are in Israel? Where are there shopping malls? What is it like to live in Israel?)* Consider asking your educational director, rabbi, or an Israeli teacher or member of the community to visit your class and answer your students' questions.

Page 114 **The Israeli Flag:** Read aloud the text in the orange box. *(Students should underline the center star and circle the one on the right. Possible names for the Israeli flag include: David's Flag; Israel Forever.)*

Photo Op: Point to the photograph and read the caption aloud. Tell students that many people write notes with prayers or wishes and place them in the cracks of the Western Wall. On a sheet of butcher paper, draw lines to represent the stones of the Wall. Invite students to write their wishes for Israel on the stones. If you know someone who will be visiting Israel soon and is willing to bring notes to the Wall, have students write their wishes on small notes to be inserted into the cracks of the Wall.

Page 115

Photo Op: Point to the drawing of the train and read aloud the text in the orange circle. The Hebrew word for "train" is on the bottom right. The Hebrew on top of the poster means, "Have a pleasant trip on a clean train." The words on the bottom mean, "Train of Israel Limited."

Page 116

Yom Ha'atzma'ut Riddle: Have students read the riddle and the story on the blue background. Call on a volunteer to answer the riddle. *(aliyah, to go up)* Remind students that *aliyah* is the same word we use for going up to the Torah.

Sticker Time: Ask students to choose the Yom Ha'atzma'ut sticker (Israeli flag) from the back of the book and place it in the correct spot on page 11.

Chapter Review

Word Game: Write each of the seven Yom Ha'atzma'ut Dictionary words on an individual index card. Write each of the word meanings on separate index cards. In class, give each student one card. Depending on the number of students in your class, you may need to add or delete vocabulary. Challenge students to walk around the room and find the classmate who has their matching card. After all matches have been found, invite students to read aloud the words and their meanings.

Yom Ha'atzma'ut Word Puzzle: Have student partners complete the puzzle. Challenge students to circle all the Hebrew words on the puzzle page. *(Eretz Yisrael—three times; Hatikvah; Medinat Yisrael, and aliyah)* The answers to the puzzle are as follows: BIBLE, ZIONISM, STAR, HATIKVAH, HERZL, ALIYAH, ISRAEL.

Holiday Journal: Have students write about or illustrate what they would most like to do on a visit to Israel.

Family Activity: For fun, have families identify Israeli items in their homes. They might, for example, have ḥummus in the refrigerator, a ḥanukkiyah or mezuzah made in Israel, or tomatoes grown in Israel. Consider asking students to share this information in class. List all items on the board.

CHAPTER 13

שָׁבוּעוֹת

Shavuot

Textbook pages 118–126

Chapter Overview

Rivkah and Daniel learn that on Shavuot we read the Ten Commandments, celebrate the giving of the Torah, eat dairy foods like blintzes and cheesecake, and remember how the Israelites brought their first fruits to the Holy Temple each year at this time.

Getting Started

Ask open-ended questions about rules, such as: What are some rules we have in our classroom? *(raising your hand)* What are some rules you have at home? *(respect my parents)* When do you set rules? *(when playing a game)* Why and when is it important to have rules? Guide students to understand that rules are needed to help keep people safe and to ensure that actions are carried out fairly. Tell students that they are going to learn about Shavuot, a holiday in which we celebrate the most famous set of rules: the Ten Commandments.

Core Concept

On Shavuot, we remember the importance of honoring the Torah and doing *mitzvot*, and we celebrate the early summer harvest.

Learning Objectives

Students will be able to:

- Identify and explain the four names of Shavuot.
- Describe Shavuot customs, such as eating dairy foods.
- Retell some of the biblical events that have to do with the receiving of the Ten Commandments.
- Discuss the importance of performing *mitzvot* and helping others.

Teaching Opportunities

Page 118

Hebrew Month Song: Call on a volunteer to read the date. *(6th of Sivan)* If your students created Hebrew month songs, invite a volunteer to lead the class in singing one of the songs.

Photo Op: Ask: What do you see in this picture? *(a parade)* What do you think the boy is pulling? *(Answers will vary.)* Guide students to understand that the boy is pulling a prop that represents Moses going up Mount Sinai and the Jewish people being given the Torah, including the Ten Commandments. Ask students how the boy might be feeling as he is walking in this parade. *(proud to be Jewish; happy to be walking in the parade; proud of the prop he helped make)* Tell students that on Shavuot we celebrate God's giving the Torah to the Jewish people.

Page 119

Torah Acrostic: Have students write an acrostic poem about the Torah using the letters of TORAH to begin each line. A sample acrostic might read: **T**eaches us how to live as Jews/ **O**ver thousands of years old/ **R**ead all over the world/ **A**nswers many of our questions/ **H**elps us be better people.

Page 120

Photo Op: Point to the photograph at the top of the page and ask the question in the caption in the green circle. *(Answers may include: It makes me feel good when I make others happy; my brother acts nicer to me when I am nice to him.)* Ask: What are some ways you show love and kindness to members of your family? *(read to a younger sibling; play a card game with a grandparent; help cook dinner)*

HANDS ON

Hands On: Teach, or have your cantor or music specialist teach, your students to sing *"Torah tzivah lanu Moshe."* Explain that these words mean "Moses commanded the Torah to us" and are from the morning prayer service. For fun, have your students form a circle and dance a "Mayim step" (see page 23 of this Teacher's Guide) as they sing.

***Mitzvot* List:** Divide the class into groups of four to five students. Ask groups to list all the *mitzvot* they can think of in the next three minutes. *(Answers may include: lighting Shabbat candles; learning about the Torah; giving tzedakah; being kind to animals.)* After three minutes, have a reporter from each group read its list of *mitzvot*. For fun, count how many different *mitzvot* your class was able to list.

Page 121

Counting the Omer: Refer to a Jewish calendar, or find an omer calendar on the Internet, and tell students what number day of the omer it is today. Your educational director or rabbi could help you locate this information. Continue to count the omer with your students each time you meet prior to Shavuot. You may wish to post a chart or omer calendar for students to cross off the days of the omer.

Four Names for Shavuot: Give each student a sheet of construction paper. Ask students to fold the paper into four equal rectangles and to write one of the names of Shavuot in each quadrant. *(Shavuot; Ḥag Hakatzir; Ḥag Habikkurim; Zeman Matan Torataynu)* Invite students to illustrate each of the names. For example, students might draw a seven-week calendar, people harvesting wheat, a basket of fruits, and Mount Sinai with the Ten Commandments.

Counting the Days and Weeks: Read aloud the text in the orange box and guide students to fill in the blanks. *(Responses may include: counting the days to a birthday or vacation; it adds excitement by reminding you of it every day; it reminds us that Shavuot is coming and helps us feel the anticipation the Israelites felt.)*

Page 122

Shavuot Blessings: Give students copies of the Shavuot blessings found at www.ElijahRocks.net. Review these Shavuot blessings and encourage students to practice them at home.

Photo Op: Call on volunteers to name the fruits and vegetables shown in the photograph. *(oranges; grapes; peaches; bananas; tomatoes; watermelon)* Ask which foods they would like to taste. Tell students that the sign in front, with the number 4, also reads "matok," meaning sweet. Encourage students to notice if *sweet* is written next to fruits at their grocery stores.

Page 123

The Book of Ruth. A children's version of the story of Ruth can be found in *The Explorer's Bible, Volume 2* (Behrman House), Chapter 7; or check the synagogue or local library for other resources.

Photo Op: Read aloud the photograph caption and ask students to name some sweet dairy foods. For fun, create a Shavuot menu of your students' favorite dairy foods. Bring in photographs of these foods, or ask students to draw them, and paste the pictures onto the menu. If possible, bring some of these foods to share with the class.

Page 124

Mount Sinai: Have students read the first three paragraphs of the story silently. Ask: What did the Israelites see and hear in this story? *(thunder; black sky; lightning; shofar blasting)* Call on volunteers to imagine that they were at Mount Sinai and to tell the rest of the class what they experienced.

Page 125

Hands On: Assign each student one of the Ten Commandments. (Depending on the size of your class, you may ask two students to work together.) Give each student a sheet of construction paper and markers. Ask students to make a mini-poster that illustrates their commandment and explains why it is important. Invite students to present their posters to the class.

Ten Commandments: If possible, have students play the Ten Commandments game at www.ElijahRocks.net, arranging the Ten Commandments in order. Encourage students to play the game with their families for fun and for additional review.

Pages 124–126

Shavuot Riddle: Read the Shavuot Riddle on page 124 and ask students to guess the answer before reading the story. List their guesses on the board. Ask students to read the whole story with a partner and to look for the answer to the riddle. *(Honor the Torah and God by doing mitzvot.)*

Sticker Time: Ask students to choose the Shavuot sticker (Ten Commandments) from the back of the book and place it in the correct spot on page 11.

Chapter Review

Word Game: Write each Shavuot Dictionary word and phrase (found at www.ElijahRocks.net) on a separate sheet of paper. Invite a student to the front of the room and tape one of the words or phrases to the student's back. Ask the student to turn around and show classmates the word or phrase. Have the student ask classmates for up to five clues and then try to guess the word or phrase. Have students take turns coming to the front of the room to guess a Shavuot word or phrase.

Shavuot Word Puzzle: Give students copies of the puzzle found at www.ElijahRocks.net. Have student partners complete the puzzle. Ask students to write two more puzzle sentences about Shavuot. *(Example: The Israelites received the Ten Commandments at Mount __ I N A__.)* Have pairs of students exchange and solve each other's puzzles. Answers to the puzzle are as follows: SHAVUOT, OMER, HABIKKURIM, DAIRY, RUTH, TORAH.

Holiday Journal: Have students write about or illustrate a mitzvah they are proud of doing.

Family Activity: Encourage families to decide on a new mitzvah they can do together. Suggest examples such as attending synagogue services more often, inviting guests over for Shabbat dinner, or collecting coats for people who do not have homes.

Certificate of Achievement:

End of Year Party: Now that the class has successfully completed *The Jewish Holiday Treasure Trail*, prepare and sign the certificates on page 127. You may wish to plan a ceremony and invite family members, the educational director, rabbi, cantor, or any other special guests. Consider serving holiday–related snacks such as apples and honey, ḥallah, pita and hummus, or cheesecake. If your students created journals, display them proudly for guests to look at.